TRAVEL AND HO

GENERAL REFERENCE

TRAVEL AND HOLIDAY SITESEEING

How to find and arrange the perfect holiday using the Internet

Irene Krechowiecka

How To Books

Cartoons by Mike Flanagan

British Library Cataloguing in Publication Data
A catalogue record for this book is available from the British Library.

© Copyright 1998 by Irene Krechowiecka

First published by How To Books Ltd, 3 Newtec Place,
Magdalen Road, Oxford OX4 1RE, United Kingdom.
Tel: (01865) 793806. Fax: (01865) 248780.
email: info@howtobooks.co.uk
www.howtobooks.co.uk

Note: The material contained in this book is set out in good faith for
general guidance and no liability can be accepted for loss or expense
incurred as a result of relying in particular circumstances on statements
made in the book. The law and regulations may be complex and liable to
change, and readers should check the current position with the relevant
authorities before making personal arrangements.

Produced for How To Books by Deer Park Productions.
Typeset by PDQ Typesetting, Stoke-on-Trent, Staffs.
Printed and bound by Cromwell Press, Trowbridge, Wiltshire.

Contents

List of Illustrations

Preface

I am a recent convert to Internet use. For a long time I regarded it as an American fad that would probably go away if ignored. I was wrong – it will not go away and to ignore it means missing out on something that can bring real benefits to all. Whatever your interests are, you will find a wealth of information, advice and help from this global community.

This book aims to show you some of what the world has to offer the traveller and how the Internet can help you explore your own travel interests.

I would far rather spend time on the real rather than the virtual world, so have tried to keep the number of suggested sites to a minimum and highlight those resources that are efficient and effective in their delivery of worthwhile information. For me the Internet is a source of information rather than entertainment and I get impatient with sites that take a long time to load, crash my overworked computer or assail me with flashing adverts. I have as far as possible tried to avoid these, but have had to balance that with the need to present a representative picture of resources.

This book neither aims nor claims to be a comprehensive guide. Nothing written about the Internet could be. It's a medium that is constantly changing and developing. My objective is to show the possibilities and give you the ideas and techniques to make discoveries yourself.

Irene Krechowiecka

Acknowledgements

I would like to thank everyone who took the time to talk and write to me about their use of the Internet. Particular thanks go to Demon Internet for their support whilst I was writing this book, to those whose screens and site details are included in the book, to Christopher for his good natured tolerance of maternal neglect and having his computer commandeered, but most of all, to my favourite travel companion, bag carrier and proof reader.

Caveat

Every care has been taken to check the accuracy and currency of information in this book, but inevitably things will change. The author and publisher can accept no responsibility for any loss or inconvenience sustained by any reader as a result of its information or advice. Suggestions for alterations and additions can be sent to: irene.k@unforgettable.com

All product names and/or logos are trademarks of their respective owners. Their inclusion in this book does not imply endorsement of it.

1
Understanding the Internet

DISPELLING THE MYTHS

Tell someone you're writing a book and they may look politely interested. Tell them it's about the Internet and their eyes glaze over or they begin to worry about letting their children come to play with yours. The Internet receives so much publicity that everyone has an opinion on it. Those who have used it and seen what it has to offer are frequently so enthusiastic that they evoke the glazed look response in those who haven't.

The Internet has already had a profound effect on the way we communicate and that is going to continue. Its potential benefits are enormous. No matter where you live, you have access to information from all parts of the world on all subjects. Whatever you are researching you will find an unsurpassable store of information that can be accessed easily, cheaply and is always available. Like many computer based systems it's simple to use once you've mastered a few techniques.

Basic facts
The Internet:

- is a network of computers linked by the telephone system

- is a way of moving information around the world quickly and efficiently

- enables people to share information in a way that promotes understanding, allows free speech, and encourages learning and the exchange of ideas

- allows the unscrupulous to exploit others' vulnerabilities, invade their privacy and defraud them.

The information on the Internet comes from individuals and organisations; you can contribute and hence affect the way it develops and what it contains. There is no control and little censorship. This

13

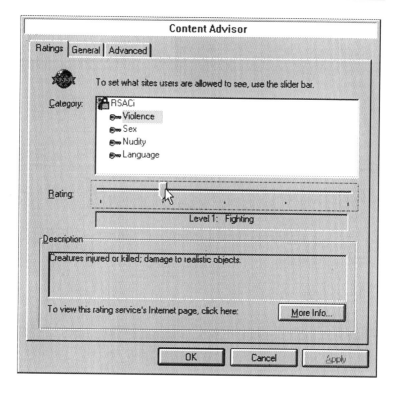

Fig. 1. Microsoft's Content Advisor.

has led to many well publicised horror stories, and indeed there is much that is truly horrible. While the Internet was an adult medium, allowing users to control it themselves worked reasonably well. As more children access the Internet, systems for protecting them have developed. In addition to making use of these, all users need to be informed about potential dangers and how to cope with them.

Internet software allows you to regulate what is made available to users. The most basic form of control is contained in some browser software, such as Microsoft's Content Advisor on Internet Explorer (see Figure 1). A range of additional, more sophisticated, filtering software is available. This is described and evaluated in the sites listed at the end of this chapter, which are maintained by organisations working to make the Internet a safe and positive experience for all users.

EXPLOITING THE POTENTIAL

Worries about the Internet should not prevent you from seeing for yourself what it has to offer. That which is good far exceeds that which is not. This book identifies and describes worthwhile sites and shows techniques for finding more for yourself.

The benefits of Internet access

Internet access gives you the opportunity to:

☑ access up-to-date information anywhere in the world
☑ research subjects in great depth
☑ make connections you'd not previously thought of
☑ make contact with others who share your interests
☑ inform about what is good and warn about what is bad
☑ explore new subjects and possibilities
☑ obtain free newsletters that keep you up to date with offers and travel news
☑ find travelling companions
☑ publish your own travel tales
☑ plan and book your travel from home
☑ find 'what's on' in most places in the world
☑ investigate hazards in your chosen holiday area
☑ compare price and special offers efficiently
☑ check weather and traffic conditions
☑ look at places through live cameras
☑ look at or buy maps and guidebooks that may otherwise be difficult to obtain.

TRUE OR FALSE?

It costs a lot in phone calls.
False. If used discriminatingly it can be a cheap way of obtaining information. When you connect to the Internet you do so for the cost of a local phone call. How much that costs depends on how long you stay connected. If you know what you are doing and what you are looking for it's possible to get information very quickly. This book aims to show you how and where to do just that. For more detailed information see Chapter 9.

It takes ages to get anything off the web.
True and false. The time it takes to transfer information depends on a

number of factors which are explained in Chapter 9, where you will also find suggestions for speeding things up.

You will be inundated with junk mail.
False. People can only mail you if they know your address, and you can choose who you give that to.

You need all the latest equipment and that's out of date as soon as you buy it.
False. You can access the Internet using software and hardware that is a few years old. Computers and Internet software are developing all the time. It's almost impossible for the ordinary user to keep up to date, and in many ways it doesn't matter. You may not see latest features, but if it's good information you want, you can still get it. A faster computer can speed up data transfer. The best ways to avoid spending on equipment that may get out of date is to use public Internet facilities.

There's too much information and no easy way of getting what you want.
False. It is confusing at first because there is almost limitless information. However, there are ways of finding what you want, and they are all explained in this book.

People can misuse your credit card if you make financial transactions on the web.
True. You should never send credit card details through insecure sites or via e-mail. However, on secure sites a credit card transaction is as safe as it would be over the telephone. There is more information later in this chapter.

It's unsafe to let your children use the web.
False. There are sites on the web that you would not want children to see, just as there are books, films and magazines. There is much for children to learn and discover through Internet use. In relation to travel, it's good to involve them in researching and planning family holidays and school trips. There is software that can help you control your children's use of the Internet and you have to teach them to use common sense and act safely. It's a form of communication that's here to stay, so share its wonders with them. Place your computer in a family room rather than a bedroom; by making it a family activity you can keep an eye on things.

It can infect your computer with viruses.
True. You should have an up-to-date virus checker. Most computers come with one, but the software needs to be updated regularly.

People can pretend to be something they are not.
True. You should always take sensible precautions before divulging personal information, parting with money or arranging to meet someone you've written to. Sites which offer guidelines on Internet safety can be found at the end of the chapter.

You have to pay for access to quality information.
False. All the sites listed in this book provide free access. There are thousands of people who have something worthwhile to contribute to any debate on any subject for totally non-commercial reasons. There are, for example, whole travel books made freely available.

You can find the answer to just about any question.
True. Just try posting a difficult question to the relevant newsgroup!

People are very helpful on the web.
True. Although there are weirdos, con men and eccentrics out there, the most positive thing about the Internet is its spirit of sharing and co-operation.

You can find cheap holidays.
True. You can also find unusual ones and things right on your doorstep that you'd not previously thought of.

All this will put travel agents out of business.
False. Many independent travel agencies have seen a dramatic increase in business because of the Internet. They can make their expertise and services available to a much larger audience than through their shops. Many travellers use the web to research their options, get an idea of price and then use a travel agent to make the final arrangements. Travel agents can help you more if you've done your research first, and are sometimes able to offer you the same for less as they have access to offers that are not generally available.

You can communicate with people anywhere in the world for the cost of a local phone call.
True. If you both have an e-mail connection. For more information on this see Chapter 9.

It opens up possibilities you had not previously thought of.
True. The links that characterise web sites may lead you into trains of thought which wouldn't otherwise have occurred to you. You can also read about other people's travels, disasters or adventures and in many cases communicate directly with them.

All this information is available elsewhere, there's no need to use the Internet.
False. Much of the information in the sites listed in this book is *only* available via the Internet. Where the same information can be obtained elsewhere it's often cheaper, easier and faster to use the Internet. National Tourist Information Offices, for example, have comprehensive web sites where you can quickly find the information *you* want. Their phone service, on the other hand, is often automated and at expensive call rates. The long number of options that you get rarely includes one that answers your query. The result is general information. Which in turn means more calls, letters and delays until you get what you need.

MAKING USE OF SAFEGUARDS

Personal safety

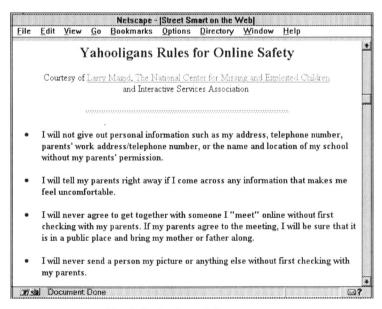

Fig. 2. Rules for safe Internet use.

The Internet is both personal and anonymous. The people you communicate with can hide or protect their identity behind an e-mail address, and so can you. There is no problem until you start to divulge personal details. Take the usual precautions you would when dealing with any stranger (see Figure 2 for advice aimed at children but applicable to all). Remember that people online may not be who they seem. Because you can't see or hear the person it would be easy for someone to misrepresent him or herself. Thus, someone indicating that 'she' is a '14-year-old girl' could in reality be a 50-year-old man.

If you are aware of the dangers, you can make Internet use safe for yourself and your children. If you come across something that offends you, close it down. You don't have to read it or look at it.

Financial safety

Anyone can set up a web site and claim to be whatever takes their fancy. Sites related to travel number millions. Some belong to commercial companies, some to individuals or educational institutions who want to share rather than sell their knowledge. Amongst these are dishonest operations and individuals. It's up to you to examine the information critically, check that the companies you deal with are legitimate and that any money you part with is safe.

Don't be taken in by the appearance of the site – a good looking site is no guarantee of quality information or product. Many of the best sites have relatively plain interfaces. Reputable travel companies and tour operators will display the logo of regulatory associations they belong to and give details of safeguards offered.

Buying from the web

Financial transactions on the web should only be carried out on secure sites. Browsers such as Explorer and Navigator use SSL (Secure Sockets Layer) which encrypts the data you send so no one can read or change it during transmission (see Figure 3). You can send your credit card number to a secure site with as much safety as giving your details over the phone. Secure sites have an unbroken key or padlock symbol and the URL (Uniform Resource Locator) starts with https (see Chapter 8). Secure sites don't remove all the risks. You are trusting the server administrator with your credit card number and no technology can protect you from dishonest or careless people. One great advantage of paying by credit card is that if you do not get the services or goods you paid for you will be reimbursed. *This does not apply to transactions using debit cards such as Switch*. Some travel companies impose small surcharges for payments made by credit card.

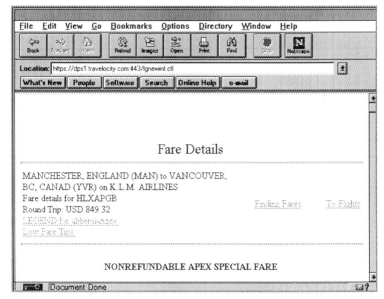

Fig. 3. Example of a secure site.

Commercial fraud that existed before the Internet exists on it. New technologies enable new ways of perpetrating fraud. The US-based Internet Fraud Watch service helps consumers distinguish between legitimate and fraudulent promotions. It provides tips, articles, bulletins and other information to help users avoid fraud and protect their privacy.

Safeguards for travellers

In most countries there are organisations which represent travel agents and protect travellers. In the UK they are AITO (Association of Independent Tour Operators) and ABTA (Association of British Travel Agents). Member agencies display the logo of the organisation and have a registration number. Membership means:

- the company is financially sound
- the descriptions in their brochures are accurate
- they will handle your booking in accordance with predetermined standards of service and quality
- your money is safe
- you will never be stranded abroad.

Understanding ATOL
There are additional safeguards covering the purchase of air tickets. In the UK any company selling air travel is required by law to hold an Air Traffic Organiser's Licence (ATOL), issued by the Civil Aviation Authority (CAA). If you pay any money – even a deposit – to a travel firm for a flight or a package holiday by air, the sale must be protected by an ATOL, unless you get a valid air ticket straight away. If a company does not have its own ATOL it must book you with one that does and give you a receipt showing which ATOL you are covered by. This only applies to flights booked in and originating from the UK, though other countries operate similar systems. Companies normally display the ATOL logo and a four digit registration number. ATOL cover means:

- If your travel firm goes broke whilst you're on holiday, all the things included in your holiday will be paid for and you'll be brought home at the end.

- If your operator goes broke before you leave, you will get a full refund or be offered an alternative holiday.

- You'll normally be covered for a scheduled flight if the airline fails. ATOL holders can opt out of this, but only if they clearly state on your documents that you are not covered for scheduled airline failure.

During 1997-8, the CAA enabled 20,000 people to complete their holidays after their tour operator had failed and gave refunds to 73,000 people who would otherwise have lost their money.

Judging the standard and accuracy of information
Accuracy of information has always been something that has aroused discussion in the context of marketing travel and tourism. Although there is increased regulation of descriptions in brochures, travel and tourist information providers want to promote their area or product, so they make everywhere sound wonderful.

The web gives access to a greater range of both official and unofficial information from every country in the world, so standards are bound to vary. It's up to you to check the accuracy of the information and be discriminating. You should:

- be aware that marketing material is always flattering

- use live web cameras where possible rather than relying on carefully constructed photographs

- use news and discussion groups to ask others who have been to the same country/resort/accommodation for details of their experiences

- use e-mail to question travel companies about aspects you would like to have clarified

- Use a variety of information sources, *eg* news and discussion groups, travel book updates, travelogues.

You can find non-promotional information from local newspapers, educational institutions and from people who publish their travel experiences on the Internet. In real life you would speak to someone who has been where you're planning to go. Using the Internet you can do this through travel or country related newsgroups.

CASE STUDIES

Tom tries a free Internet trial
Tom needed little persuasion to buy one of the latest computers as a Christmas present for his children. He is not totally convinced by their argument that Internet access would make it more educational, if only they could have it, like everybody else at school. Tom decides to try it for a limited period as a free trial won't cost him much, but wonders if giving his children unrestricted access to the Internet will cause problems. He's reassured by the service provider that their software will enable him to regulate how his children use the Internet.

Chris worries about the future
One of the things Chris knows he will miss most when he leaves university is his free Internet access. He's used it to keep in touch with all his friends, and to arrange some excellent bargain ski holidays, as well as for the odd bit of academic research. The law firm taking him on as a trainee is prehistoric and views the Internet with grave suspicion. It will take some time to gently persuade them of its potential. There's no way he can think of getting his own computer until he's paid off all his debts, which could take decades. He decides to investigate what's on offer in the library.

Mary joins a free computer literacy class
Mary doesn't know anything about computers and doesn't particularly want to, as she could never afford one. When the local primary school offers free classes in computing she agrees to go to keep her friend company. As soon as she has put her name down she begins to regret it. It's ages since she managed to learn anything new and she

hasn't even mastered setting the video. She's bound to make a fool of herself in front of everybody.

SITESEEING TIPS

Safe Internet use
Netparents
http://www.netparents.org
American site providing resources for parents concerned about inappropriate material online. Lots of useful content and links.

Safe Kids
http://www.safekids.com
Content and links for children, teachers, parents and others on issues related to children and the Internet. It is maintained by the American writer, Lawrence J Magid, author of *Child Safety on the Information Highway* (see Figure 2). The full text of this brochure, which puts the benefits and dangers of Internet use in perspective, is available on this site. There are evaluations of filtering software and common sense suggestions for concerned parents.

Safe Surf
http://www.safesurf.com
An organisation working at making the Internet safe for children without censorship. They have developed the Safe Surf Rating System, which you can add to Microsoft's Explorer.

Smart Parent
http://www.smartparent.com
Information on blocking and filtering software, links to parent and child-friendly sites, agencies and organisations that focus on Internet-related issues. Free electronic newsletter on child safety on the Internet.

Web Scams
http://w3.one.net/~banks/webscam.htm
Excerpts from *Web Psychos, Stalkers, and Pranksters* by Michael A Banks. Lots of useful information on how to avoid trouble.

World Village
http://www.worldvillage.com/wv/school/htm/control.htm
Believes that empowering and educating parents rather than imposing censorship is the key to protecting children on the Internet. This

section of the site gives details of companies involved in finding ways to keep the Internet safe. Much of the software described can be downloaded.

Financial safety
ABTA
http://www.abtanet.com
ABTA bonded tour operators and travel agencies are responsible for the sale of over 90 per cent of package holidays in the UK. Details of ABTA's standards and other useful travel related information on this site.

US Federal Trade Commissions
http://www.ftc.gov
Type 'Internet scams' into the search box on this site to link to leaflets and reports which highlight what needs to be looked out for and avoided.

USA National Fraud Information Center (NFIC)
http://www.fraud.org
Internet Fraud Watch was created in 1996 to offer consumers advice about promotions in cyberspace and facilitate reporting of suspected Internet fraud. As Internet commerce is global, this site has useful information for all Internet users.

Visa and Mastercard
http://www.visa.com
http://www.mastercard.com
These two major credit card companies have devoted considerable space on their sites to reassuring consumers about the safety of Internet commerce. Both sites have demos and descriptions of how it all works and, not surprisingly, try to persuade you how wonderful shopping via the Internet is.

2
The Internet and Travel

CHOOSING THE RIGHT HOLIDAY

Holidays are a significant highlight in our lives. We look forward to them and spend a substantial amount on them. Some turn out to be better than hoped for, others are a disaster. Most disasters could be avoided by good research and preparation and the Internet makes this easy. Good information helps you make good choices. Before you start investigating all the options you need an idea of what is important to you and those you are travelling with.

What can I do on holiday?
Do you want to lie in the sun and do nothing, or take the time to learn, eat, see or try out something new? You can, of course, do a bit of both. Chapter 3 has detailed information on using the Internet to research activity holidays.

How do I keep everyone happy?
Trying to live up to the dreams and expectations of a diverse range of people is not easy. Many family holidays are disasters because, by trying to please everyone, they please no one. Just because you share the same genes does not mean you will enjoy the same holiday. As a general rule if your children are happy so will you be, if they're miserable they'll make sure you are too. The web makes it easy to involve every member of the group in researching the different possibilities a particular destination can offer. Get each person to make a 'wish list' and investigate it using the web. If they're short on ideas they can read a few travelogues or browse through travel related sites. It's even possible to ask the whole world a question about it: Figure 4 shows an extract from Lonely Planet's Thorn Tree section, a place for discussion and questions. The questions used are are taken from 'kids to go' and 'women travellers'. Readers are invited to respond or start their own discussions.

Saltspring Island Created by: Christopher	Travelling with children Created by: Susanne
	Hi there! In a weeks time me and my two girls aged 5 and 7 are leaving for Thailand and Malaysia. We will be gone for 6 weeks, ending up and flying back from Singapore. As I am not a very experienced traveller the nervousness has set in and I wonder about a lot of things. We will start with two days in Bangkok (with a prebooked hotel), after that I plan to go to Ciang Mai. Does anybody know of fun activities for children in the Ciang Mai area? They are too small for trekking, I believe, but I promised them some wildlife somehow. After Ciang Mai I do not really have any fixed plans but am thinking of flying down to Ko Samui and see some beaches and the sea. After that I do not know. If anybody out there has experience from travelling to the area with children, please let me hear from you! I have heard that the Thais love kids so I am not nervous about that, rather where to go to do childlike things.
Hello, I'm 11 years old and going on a house exchange to Saltspring Island near Vancouver with Mum and Dad this summer. I need ideas for what I might like to do there, on Vancouver Island and on the mainland.	
We have five weeks, they like to hike but always ask what I would like to do. Thing is I don't really know cos I don't know what's there. Any ideas? I like most things, even hiking!	
Thanks Chris	
[Posts on this topic: 4. Latest post: Mon 30 March, 12:40].	
Follow this topic or add your own post.	
	Hope to hear from you! Susanne

Fig. 4. Discussion from Lonely Planet's web site.

Should I stay at home or go abroad?
People often feel that they have to get as far away as they can afford to have a proper holiday. It's surprising how few people visit the attractions within an hour's travelling time that others come half way

round the world to see. Most localities now have web sites that enable you to look at what's around you with a fresh eye.

What's the best way of travelling?
Choosing the best means of transport to your destination can make or break your holiday. Driving there is not always the cheapest or best way. Map reading arguments, queues, difficulties over parking and driving on the wrong side of the road can all help give holidays that special 'wish I was at home' quality. Car breakdowns in a country where you have a less than excellent command of the language are the essential ingredient in a true holiday nightmare. If you have small children, and are facing long ferry trips or a large distance to cover in a short time, then flying is worth investigating. Air fares often compare favourably with the cost of petrol, ferries and extra break-down insurance. Sitting in an air-conditioned cabin, drinking a gin and tonic five miles *above* Belgium rather than sweltering in a five mile motorway queue *in* Belgium feels good. Detailed information on every form of transport is available on the web. This usually includes timetables, prices, special offers, and online booking facilities. See Chapter 5.

How long does it take to get there?
There is a trend for short exotic breaks, but you have to wonder if it's worth it. A weekend break to New York from the UK, for example, could mean a weekend of sleeping somewhere different for the easily fatigued. A seven-night ski holiday to the western United States from Britain will involve around a total of 16 hours' flying time and the effects of jet lag. In general it's probably better to save places that require longer travel time for longer stays so that feeling tired takes up a smaller proportion of your holiday time.

When is the best time to go?
Many people are restricted to school holiday times, which accounts for the remarkable jump in prices when families can go together. If you can escape from the tyranny of this you will find cheaper holidays, less crowded resorts, even more acceptable weather. Holiday resorts can have a wonderful feel about them off season. Holiday periods vary considerably across the world. The long summer break in New Zealand is in January, and it feels as if the whole of Europe is travelling to ski resorts in February. Details of national holiday dates are easily found on the web.

What sort of accommodation should I look for?
There are web sites that search for accommodation across the whole range of options from luxury hotels to camp grounds. Hotels and hotel chains have their own sites, organisations for walkers, climbers and cyclists often provide links to accommodation details on their sites. Conservation organisations like the National Trust and Vivat have schemes which allow holidaymakers to stay in their properties. 'Stay free' schemes such as home or hospitality exchange could give a new dimension to your travels and are described in more detail in Chapter 4.

Might it be too hot?
If you're British you probably go on holiday for better weather, but if a place is too hot, it's hard to do anything other than collapse in the shade. Many visitors come to Britain in the summer because they are escaping the heat of their own country. They find our moderate temperatures ideal for walking, sightseeing, cycling and other activities, whilst we swelter in their cities. You can use the web to do detailed research on weather conditions in most parts of the world.

Might it be too cold ?
Cold places are usually chosen by holidaymakers who want particular activities. The Internet gives you access to information that helps you choose the right destination for your needs, and highlights the essential preparation and precautions. Many people who take children skiing, for example, do not realise just how cold it can get. Temperatures of –15°C are not unusual at high altitudes. If there's a wind, or the resort has a lot of long chair lifts, it's more than most children can cope with. You can use the Internet to find all this out *before* you go.

Will it be crowded?
Holidaymakers now travel to a wider range of destinations in an attempt to get away from it all, and consequently make that harder to achieve. As soon as anyone writes about a quiet haven of tranquillity, it's in danger of being overwhelmed by all the seekers of quiet havens of tranquillity. Some popular attractions use their web sites to show potential visitors their quietest and busiest times. Environmentally sensitive areas may operate restricted access for visitors: details and booking facilities for these can often be found on the Internet.

What will be going on when I'm there?
Huge *What's On* guides are available on the web. You can check what the big and small events will be and decide whether that makes a destination more or less attractive.

Should I stick to places I know or go somewhere new?
The problem with returning to places you've been before is that they are sometimes not as good as you remember. There is something special about doing or seeing something for the first time that can never really be duplicated. When you've been on holiday you generally remember the best times. Places change, particularly holiday resorts. The beautiful view from your balcony could now be obscured by new buildings, the cosy restaurant nobody else seemed to know about may have become a burger bar... use the Internet to update your memories and then decide if it's worth a revisit.

I don't like to feel that I'm harming others or the environment by the holidays I take.
This is a subject that has aroused much debate. If you're concerned about the impact your holiday may be having, there are places to find detailed and thoughtful information on this issue. You can also find details of holidays that make a positive contribution to the environment.

FINDING INFORMATION

The Internet sources of information are the same as in real life, but you have quick, cheap and efficient access to more. You can research holiday types, destinations and prices and can communicate with people who've been there so you can find out what it's really like. It can take you on 'virtual visits' to exotic and expensive destinations, giving a new dimension to armchair travel. Take a tour of Antarctica for the cost of a local call!

Travel agents
A lot of agents now have a web presence and offer you the same service online as you would get if you went into their shop. If you haven't got easy access to an independent or specialist travel agent, you can find many on the web, as well as all the big companies.

Travel magazines

There are several on the web, some of which are aimed at particular interest groups. Many can be obtained through a free e-mail subscription.

Travellers' tales

From Homer and Chaucer to present-day travel shows, others' experiences are fascinating. Many travel web sites include travelogues and discussion groups where you can read the work of others or contribute a travel story of your own.

Travel books

Travel book publishers' sites are amongst some of the best for detailed up-to-date information. They commonly make extracts and even whole books available on their sites, so keeping their printed material up to date. Some authors choose to publish only on the web, particularly on subjects that publishers may consider too specialist to be commercially viable.

GETTING A BARGAIN

Many people choose their holidays on price rather than destination. Travel companies appear to have an endless supply of special deals and offers. The Internet gives easy access to information on these and helps you compare details. There are sites, mailing lists and newsgroups devoted to holiday promotions, as well as an abundance of advice and ideas on budget travel from travellers. In addition to sites listed at the end of this chapter, information for bargain hunters can be found in Chapters 5 and 9.

Some of the cheapest holidays are those booked at the last minute, but you take the risk that you might not get anything at all! The closer to departure time you leave it, the cheaper the holiday gets. Because the Internet allows fast and effective communication it's an excellent tool for finding and booking a last minute holiday. When looking at 'bargains' you need to check for hidden extra costs such as booking fees, insurance and credit card surcharges.

Using teletext

TV-based teletext does not incur any phone charges but the web version has certain advantages (see Figure 5):

☑ It's much quicker, each web page shows around six teletext pages.

Fig. 5. One of the best UK sources of late holiday information is teletext.

☑ You don't have problems of a poor signal making information difficult to read.

☑ The web pages have details of the last update so you can see if offers are current.

☑ It's easy to find and use the 'title' page which explains all the abbreviations.

☑ You can print details or take as long as you like looking at them offline.

☑ It's easier to compare offers, taking into account extra costs such as booking or credit card charges.

☑ You have a record of the company's ABTA or ATOL registration.

SORTING OUT SPECIAL NEEDS

Travel for people with disabilities presents special concerns. There are many excellent sites on the web which aim to make travel an enjoyable and trouble free experience for those who might otherwise not leave home. These can be personal sites or a part of tourist information, government or broadcasting web sites. The Internet allows disabled travellers to share their information and expertise freely. General newsgroups for people with disabilities also give an opportunity for travel related issues to be discussed. This helps raise awareness of the issues and promote accessible travel.

ATTRACTION ACCESSIBILITY LIST

Magic Kingdom Park

Guests must transfer from wheelchair to board the following attractions:

- Walt Disney World Railroad (Main Street Station)
- Main St. Transportation
- Jungle Cruise
- Pirates of the Caribbean
- Swiss Family Treehouse
- Big Thunder Mountain Railroad -- health, age, and size are considerations
- Splash Mountain -- health, age, and size are considerations
- Tom Sawyer Island
- The Haunted Mansion
- Mike Fink Keelboats
- Cinderella's Golden Carrousel
- Dumbo the Flying Elephant
- Mad Tea Party
- Mr. Toad's Wild Ride
- Peter Pan's Flight

Fig. 6. Disney's site explains their facilities for disabled visitors.

CASE STUDIES

Tom finds a bargain break

After yet another cold and wet weekend Tom decides to have a look at holiday availability for the following week, which is the children's half term. The offers are so tempting that he decides to book a flight to Spain with a self catering apartment and car hire for just under £500. He then uses the web to investigate the possibilities offered by Andalucia and is pleasantly surprised by the number of mountain walks that are available within driving distance of the Costa del Sol.

Chris makes plans for his parents

Chris's parents are taking early retirement and intend to spend a year travelling. They need to investigate affordable ways of doing this. Chris uses the Internet to help and comes up with lots of different ideas including hospitality exchanges and details of work teaching English abroad as a boost for flagging funds.

Mary does a project on York

Mary's course has done wonders for her confidence. She now finds it hard to believe that she was ever daunted by a computer. As part of a project using the Internet she decides to research a holiday she's been planning in York. She's worried about the cost and arranges for her children to look at the web sites of places they want to visit. These include the National Railway Museum (**http://www.nmsi.ac.uk**) and the Jorvik Centre (**http://www.jorvik-viking-centre.co.uk**). She tells them what her budget for entry costs is and lets them decide how to spend it. She finds links to all the tourist sites from York City Council's site (**http://www.york gov.uk/heritage/index.html**).

SITESEEING TIPS

More sites that will help you plan your trip and investigate what is right for you are listed at the end of Chapters 3, 5 and 7.

Bookshops

Search quickly through huge stocks, order online, read or even write reviews. You will often find advertising links to bookshops on travel sites. Examples include:

Amazon: **http://www.amazon.com**
Barnes and Noble: **http://www.barnesandnoble.com**
Dillons: **http://www.dillons.co.uk**
Internet Bookshop: **http://www.bookshop.co.uk**
Waterstones: **http://www.waterstones.co.uk**
World Traveller Books & Maps: **http://www.avantamedia.com**

Travel books and publishers

Frommers
http://www.frommers.com
Two hundred cities and islands account for more than 80 per cent of all vacation travel, so Frommers concentrate on providing detailed information on those in their *Outspoken Encyclopaedia of Travel*. A nice feature of the site is the hospitality exchange section (see Chapter 4).

Lonely Planet
http://www.lonelyplanet.com
A goldmine of practical down to earth information for all travellers. Lonely Planet's own content is of excellent quality. The external links are comprehensive, well maintained and logically organised. An added bonus is 'Text Express', a fast and beautifully simple version of the site for those who are concerned about online times.

Moon Travel Books
http://www.moon.com
Publishers of travel handbooks. Site has excellent information and updated links to all the Internet resources mentioned in *The Practical Nomad: How to Travel Around the World*, which they publish. Facility to order books online.

Rough Guides
http://www.roughguides.com
Publishers of well known travel and other guides. This site contains reader updates for published books and details of all their titles. They have a second site:
http://hotwired.com/rough
which, in theory, gives access to the full text of some of their guides and is searchable.

The Art of Travel
http://www.artoftravel.com
John Gregory wrote *How to See the World The Art of European and World Travel Backpacking on $25 a Day or Less* 'because too many people are missing the experience of world travel, mainly because they don't realise how easy, fun, and economical it is to pack a bag and just go.' He was appalled at how little publishers were willing to pay and decided to make it freely available on the Internet. You can download the whole book (25 chapters, 80,000 words, and 120 illustrations) and read it at your leisure. It's got something for all types of travellers.

The Electronic Traveler
http://www.infotec-travel.com
The first directory of travel information on the Internet, originally published in 1994, is now available and regularly updated on the web. The author, Marcus Endicott, is the founder and moderator of Green Travel and Infotec-travel mailing lists, both well worth subscribing to. Details of how to do that are on the Infotec site and in Chapter 9.

Travel magazines
Many travel related sites have online magazines. Examples include: *Journeywoman* (aimed at women travellers).
http://www2.journeywoman.com/journeywoman

The Planet (Electronic Telegraph's travel section).
http://www.the-planet.co.uk

Travel Insight
http://www.a2btravel.com/travelinsight

Vapor Trails
http://www.vaportrails.com

E-mail magazines are also available free of charge. See how to subscribe to these in Chapter 9.

Finding a bargain
All the Gateway Sites in Chapter 7 have details of holiday offers and promotions. Cheap deals on fares can be found in sites listed at the end of Chapter 5.

Bargain Holidays
http://www.bargainholidays.com
A searchable database of holidays from the UK. Lots of useful links to other travel related matters from this site.

Teletext
http://www.teletext.co.uk
Excellent source of information on cheap holidays from the UK.

Accommodation
AccomoDATA
http://www.accomodata.co.uk
UK hotels, bed & breakfast, cottage and boat rentals. Searchable database and online booking.

Accommodation Search Engine
http://ase.net
A searchable database of hotels, motels, hostels, self catering and bed & breakfast accommodation worldwide. Search criteria include price, accommodation type, facilities and activities, which can all be arranged in order of importance. Online booking is available.

Hotel Guide
http://www.hotelguide.com
Searchable database of over 60,000 hotels, motels, resorts and bed and breakfasts. There are plans to add a currency converter, weather, maps, and destination information. Based in Switzerland but covers the world.

LeisureHunt
http://www.leisurehunt.com
Searchable database of UK tourist attractions and accommodation providers including camp sites.

Mountain Bothies Association
http://www.ma.hw.ac.uk/mba
A Scottish charity which organises the maintenance of these shelters for the benefit of all who appreciate wild and lonely places. Bothies are simple, unlocked shelters whose owners allow their use by walkers and climbers. They can be found in the Scottish Highlands and some parts of England and Wales. Information on how to find, use and participate in the upkeep of bothies.

Mountain Huts International
http://www.adventure.ch/MHI/mhi.htm
Links to many European alpine huts. Details can also be found through some of the mountaineering organizations listed in Chapter 3.

The National Trust
http://www.nationaltrust.org.uk
Basic information available on this new web site.

OffWorld Industries
http://www.vivat.org.uk
The Vivat Trust was established in 1981 as a non-profit making charitable trust to 'secure for the future benefit of the nation, buildings of historical, architectural and industrial interest that are threatened by neglect, insensitive alteration or ultimately, with demolition'. The houses they have restored are used as holiday rentals.

UK Camping and Caravanning Directory
http://camping.uk-directory.com
Resource for camping and caravanning enthusiasts in the United Kingdom. Includes a searchable database of campsites, lists of camping gear retailers, international links and the chance to chat with other enthusiasts around the world. The site's search facility allows you to enter specific criteria to help find a place that meets all your needs. These include fishing available, children's play area, suitable for wheelchairs or cycles for hire.

Special Needs
Access Able
http://www.access-able.com
The authors started this site as a result of their own experience and provide practical information for travellers wanting to 'cross town or go around the world'. The searchable database contains information on access, accommodation, and adventure holidays. Possibilities include scuba safaris, sailing, raft trips, and even a place where you can learn to sky sail. Users are encouraged to become involved in expanding the site's information. There is a text only version, a discussion forum and a selection of related links.

Disney
http://www.disney.com
A good example of a tourist attraction that has thought about the needs of disabled visitors. There is specific information for guests with sight and hearing disabilities, mobility problems, and an 'attraction accessibility list'.

Mobility International (MI)
http://europa.eu.int/geninfo/query_en.htm
The above URL takes you to a search page on the EU site. Type in 'travel and disability' and that will enable you to download pdf files on access issues in Europe. There are travel guides for tourists with disabilities covering all EU countries plus Iceland, Liechtenstein, and Norway. You will need Adobe Acrobat Reader to view these files which can be downloaded free from:
http://www.adobe.com/prodindex/acrobat/download.html

Mobility International USA (MIUSA)
http://www.miusa.org
Promotes international educational exchange, leadership development, disability rights training and travel for people with disabilities. The site invites users to 'Challenge Yourself and Change the World!' Publications include: *World of Options: A Guide to International Educational Exchange, Community Service and Travel for Persons with Disabilities, You Want To Go Where? – A Guide to China for Travellers with Disabilities and Anyone Interested in Disability Issues.*

Travelog
http://www.channel4.com/passions/travelog/main.html
Travelog is a UK travel programme in which all the presenters have a

disability. The web site contains guides to all previously featured destinations, including specific information and advice for disabled travellers. Highlights include a list of general travel resources on the web, a directory for disabled travellers, recommended further reading and specialised web sites. The 1998 destinations were Côte d'Azur, Zimbabwe, Croatia, Dublin, Beijing, The Netherlands, Vienna and India.

Ecotourism
Green Travel
http://www.green-travel.com
Dedicated to the sharing of information about culturally and environmentally responsible, or sustainable, travel and tourism worldwide, including adventure travel. Searchable site includes a World Ecotourism Directory, World Guide to Vegetarianism and the Official UNESCO Biosphere Reserve Directory. An excellent additional service is the free mailing list which carries a diverse and interesting range of information from all over the world on the impact of tourism. Details of worthwhile and unusual holidays appear here (see Figure 46).

Tourism Concern
http://www.gn.apc.org/tourismconcern
UK organisation which aims to raise awareness of and campaign on social and environmental issues related to tourism.

3
Activity Holidays

Recent research by a German doctor found that IQ dropped significantly after holidays because people did not use their brains whilst away. For some people the idea of doing nothing on holiday is the reason for going, but others find enjoyment in holidays that are busier than their normal working lives.

- Holts' Battlefield Tours Ltd Specialists in Battlefields and History: Ancient and Modern
- Golden Vision Travel Services Tours in beautiful Yorkshire
- Indian Magic Tailor-made tours for the discerning travellers to India where you can see the Real India without the rucksack!
- Internet Holidays 4 day tours of England & Scotland
- Kumuka Expeditions Overland expeditions varying from 2 - 24 weeks through Africa, South America & the Middle East. Options include white water rafting, mountaineering, diving & canoeing
- Last Frontiers Worldwide tailor-made holidays, riding, fishing, sailing & much more in exotic places
- LSG Theme Holidays Cultural Discovery holidays in both France and Britain, as well as Cookery, Bridge, Spa, Painting & Sketching and Conversational French at all levels.
- Man Around Specialist holidays for Gay and Lesbian travelers
- Midas Battlefield Tours Fully escorted tours to great battlefields of the world
- Oaktree Theatre breaks & art events in London
- Peng Travel Naturalist Holidays to Europe
- Pole Position World Motorsport Ltd Travel arrangements & tours to motor sports events world-wide
- Rainbow River Safari An eco-tour in Guyana. Camp at Marshall Falls in the 16,800 acre conservation area. Swimming, fishing, panning for gold & diamonds (!), white water rafting (on a raft you've built yourself) and much more.

Fig. 7. World Travel shows the options and
gives contacts for more detailed information.

There is an enormous number of holiday possibilities for those who want to take part in or learn a new outdoor activity. Combinations that suit you can be arranged through specialist operators independently, using information from the web and newsgroups (see Figure 7). Some areas of activity have developed a huge presence on the Internet. There is extensive information on:

- skiing
- walking
- climbing and mountaineering
- cycling.

There are many 'informal' sites related to these areas of interest which were in many cases started by individuals as students and then continued as a hobby.

SKIING

There are personal and commercial sites and several well used newsgroups related to skiing. American resorts have had a web presence for some time and the number of European resorts making information available in this way has increased rapidly in the past twelve months.

Features of ski resort web sites

- Web cameras allowing you to view live conditions.
- Weather, snow and avalanche reports and forecasts.
- Details of lifts operating.
- Information on accommodation and online booking facilities.
- Details of, and special offers for, lift passes and ski equipment with online booking.
- Road condition reports.
- Public transport details for access to resorts.
- Calendars of special events.

In addition to resort sites there are a number of electronic ski magazines and ski orientated web sites with articles, links and offers for skiers.

Weather and snow conditions are what skiers are most interested in. Some sites specialise in this. Where they have historical data it can help you decide on a suitable resort for your holiday dates (see Figure 8).

WALKING, CLIMBING AND MOUNTAINEERING

Information on these activities is provided by mountaineering clubs, ramblers associations, tourist boards, national parks and forestry

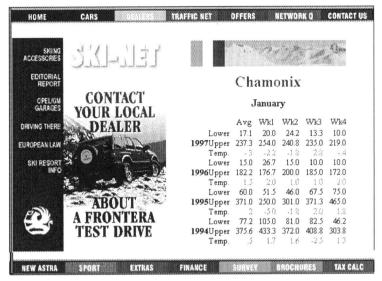

Fig. 8. Vauxhall's ski reports give temperatures
and snow depths for several years.

services and interested individuals. There are also sites devoted to
weather for walkers and climbers (see Figure 9).

You can use the Internet to:

- find maps, photographs and itineraries

- find walking companions

- look at details of new or proposed routes

- communicate with people who have done walks or climbs

- check potential hazards

- investigate details of restrictions for some ecologically sensitive
  areas

- find details of camp sites and accommodation

- find details of climbing walls.

Long distance footpaths
Long distance footpaths often cross whole countries or continents.
UK, European and American long distance paths have web sites with

links to all the information you need to plan your walk in advance, including details of companies that will transport your baggage to make things a little easier.

Many long distance footpaths are open to cyclists and horse riders, as well as walkers. The routes in remote areas are usually dotted with campsites, which in the US can include stable facilities for those doing the route on horseback! Examples of paths include:

- Pacific Crest National Scenic Trail. Canada to Mexico, through The Cascades and Sierra Nevada mountain ranges (2,638 miles).

- Oregon National Historic Trail (2,170 miles).

- Pony Express National Historic Trail (1,855 miles). The old mail route that connected the eastern United States to California.

- The Pennine Way: (251 miles: 402 km).

- Thames Path: (180 miles: 288 km).

- Offa's Dyke Path: (168 miles: 270 km).

- North Cape to Sicily (5,000 km). From Norway to Italy via Sweden, Denmark, Germany and Switzerland.

CREAG MEAGAIDH

AVALANCHE HAZARD 1500 HRS SAT

Heavy snow on very strong W winds is continuing the build up of very unstable windslab. Slopes of a NW to SE aspect above 800m are affected. The avalanche hazard is High (Category 4).

AVALANCHE HAZARD OUTLOOK SUN

Further snowfall overnight on hurricane force W winds will add to the very unstable windslab on NW to SE slopes above 800m. Avalanches will occur in these areas. Snowfalls will continue through the day on SW/SE winds adding to the current unstable conditions. A High (Category 4) hazard of avalanche will exist.

CLIMBING CONDITIONS

SNOW DISTRIBUTION: Currently, 40cm of new snow to be found at 800m.

ICING: Very poor and buried under lots of new snow.

COMMENT: This weather should help fill in the gullies, but patience is required. Very poor mountain conditions today.

Fig. 9. The Scottish Avalanche Information Service.

- Scotland to Nice (2,600 km). From Britain to France via The Netherlands, Belgium and Luxemburg, including the Grande Traversée des Alpes.

- Istanbul to Spain (7,200 km). From Turkey to Spain via Bulgaria, Romania, Hungary, Slovakia, Poland, Czech Republic, Germany, Luxemburg, Belgium and France.

- Gibraltar to Crete (5–7,000 + km, depending on variations chosen). From Gibraltar to Greece via Spain, France, Switzerland, Austria, Germany, Hungary, Romania and Bulgaria.

CYCLING

Bikes are a common form of transport in much of the world. In many European countries it's an excellent way of travelling, with numerous cycle tracks that segregate cyclists from traffic. There are no problems with parking and it's a much cooler way of getting around in the summer. Even the UK is catching up with increased provision of safe, cycle only routes. Bikes can be hired from railway stations or cycle shops in most places around the world.

Taking your bike with you is an option worth exploring. It requires

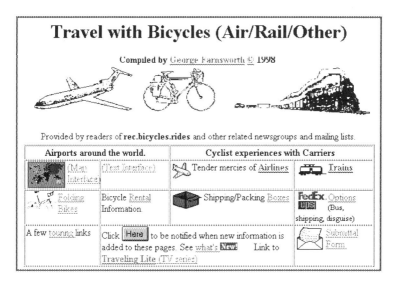

Fig. 10. George Farnsworth's site gives access to the shared wisdom of cycle related newsgroups.

careful planning but there is a web site that guides you through all the possibilities and pitfalls (see Figure 10).

As mountain biking becomes more popular, cyclists are being offered the luxury of downhill rides without the hard work of getting to the top first. The cable cars in Klosters and Davos, for example, allow bikes to be carried for a small additional payment, so you can cycle down the mountain tracks until your nerves or brake blocks give up. Not many cable car operators have web sites, but Tourist Offices do (see Chapter 7); they will be able to supply information on booking requirements and charges for bike transportation by cable car and post bus.

Other activities

Most other sporting activity holidays can be explored and arranged using the Internet including:

- archaeological exploration
- camping
- canal boating
- canoeing and kayaking
- diving
- flying
- gardening
- golf
- hang gliding
- horse riding
- hot air ballooning
- hunting
- sailing
- survival skills
- water skiing
- white water rafting
- windsurfing.

Gateway sites to all these sports are developing: a selection is listed at the end of this chapter. It's easy to find others using search engines and directories.

LEARNING AND WORKING HOLIDAYS

Historically travel provided a form of education. The European Tour, undertaken by the very rich, was a cultural and learning experience. Many travellers today use their holidays to visit or learn about historical, architectural or artistic matters. You can use the Internet to find details of tour operators who specialise in cultural and learning holidays or to make your own arrangements. You can find art galleries, museums, historical monuments, language, cookery, art and many other schools with web sites that give you all the details you need.

Museums and art galleries have made extensive use of the web, with virtual visits and preparatory material to enable you to get the most out of your actual visit.

Speciality holidays that can be researched effectively on the web include:

- learning holidays

- conservation holidays

- working holidays.

Look for more World-Wide jobs in:

- Argentina
- Australia - 5 jobs
- Austria - 1 job
- Belgium - 1 job
- Brazil - 4 jobs
- Canada - 41 jobs
- China
- Colombia - 1 job
- Denmark
- England - 2 jobs
- Egypt - 3 jobs
- Finland - 1 job
- France - 4 jobs
- Germany - 1 job
- Ghana
- Greece - 2 jobs
- Hungary
- Holland - 1 job
- India
- Ireland - 5 jobs
- Israel
- Italy - 1 job
- Japan
- Malaysia - 3 jobs
- Mexico - 2 jobs
- New Zealand
- Norway - 1 job
- Portugal
- Peoples Republic of China - 1 job
- Russia
- South Africa - 1 job
- Scotland - 1 job
- South Korea - 2 jobs
- Spain - 7 jobs
- Sweden - 1 job
- Switzerland - 2 jobs
- Thailand - 1 job
- Turkey - 9 jobs
- United Kingdom - 5 jobs
- USA - 559 jobs

Fig. 11. Summer Jobs web site.

Learning holidays
Whether it's painting, swimming, learning a new language, sailing or paragliding, it can be incorporated into your holiday.

Conservation holidays
This involves working as part of a team on a specific project in this country or abroad. Some organisations charge you for the basic cost of travel and accommodation; others cover some of your expenses.

Working holidays
Lots of sites give details of organised paid or voluntary holiday work. Many countries relax work permit requirements for holiday jobs, students, those participating in approved schemes and under 25s. Vacancies available on the search shown in Figure 11 included electro-physiologist in Austria, au pair in Finland, English teacher in China, timber feller in Lapland and plant superintendent in Colombia.

CASE STUDIES

Tom starts a new discussion in a skiing newsgroup
Tom has spent hours researching ski holidays on and off the web. It's something he used to really enjoy, but Lorna and the children aren't too sure that they'll like it. He's researched the likely weather, snow averages, travel times, ski school facilities, night life and everything else he can think of. He knows that if it doesn't work out it will all be his fault and they'll never go again. What he really wants to know is what would be a good resort for someone in his situation – the brochures and publicity make them all sound wonderful. He decides to post a question to a newsgroup and see what advice he can get. He is amazed at the response. It seems that hundreds of people want to join in the discussion he starts and he gets some really good ideas from their replies. He seems to have touched a nerve!

Chris plans his last long holiday
Chris wants to take a break between university and starting work. His future employers are happy to delay his start date, but make it quite clear that they would prefer it if he did something worthwhile. He needs something that is either very cheap or very lucrative, and wonders how he can combine that with something that will be acceptable to Creakie and Co. He turns to the web for ideas and looks at details of vacation jobs and placements. The US Internship scheme

from the Council in Europe looks promising, as do some of the jobs in Scandinavia that he finds on the Summer Jobs database.

Mary wants to learn to swim
Whilst investigating York, Mary stumbles across details of swimming classes for adults (**http://www.york.gov.uk/heritage/sport/swimming/ index.html**), something she never mastered. The class she's doing has given her confidence in her ability to learn new skills and she decides to give swimming another go.

SITESEEING TIPS

Great Outdoor Recreation Pages (GORP)
http://www.gorp.com
An excellent gateway resource for all matters related to outdoor adventures. Includes a book and map shop, accommodation information, equipment sales, bargain holidays, weather planners, information for families and camping recipes! There is detailed information on British, European and American long distance paths.

Skiing
Active Lifestyle Magazine
http://www.skifrance.com
Produce European ski- and golf-related online magazines covering Austria, Switzerland, Italy, France and North America.

1ski.com: Skiing and Snowboarding Information Service
http://www.1ski.com
Tailored to the UK skier, this site provides detailed resort guides, snow reports, holiday price and availability information for summer and winter skiing. Free e-mail newsletter in the winter ski season.

Ski France
http://www.skifrance.fr
Detailed weather and snow condition reports for all French resorts. Links to individual resorts with web sites. Not to be confused with skifrance.com above!

Ski IN
http://www.skiin.com
American-based site which claims to be the biggest information resource on skiing and snowboarding. Resort Finder covers European

as well as North American resorts. The site includes personal experiences, travel offers, online shopping for equipment and chat sessions with skiing professionals.

Skinet
http://www.skinet.com
Online American Magazine with resort and gear finder features as well as news stories, articles and links to weather reports and web cameras. Mainly North American resorts.

Ski Scotland
http://www.ski.scotland.net
This site also provides links to Scottish Tourist Board information on cycling, golf, pony trekking and fishing.

Vauxhall Skinet
http://www.vauxhall.co.uk/skinet/skititle.htm
Weather and snow reports for major European, US and Canadian ski resorts are compiled in association with The Ski Club of Great Britain. Listings can be viewed by resort or by the top ten for lower or upper snow depth. Data from previous years is included.

Walking
American National Park Service
http ://www.nps.gov/trails
Detailed information on and links to long distance footpaths in America.

Britain for Walkers
http://www.visitbritain.com
Searchable database which gives brief descriptions of a large number of routes, including long distance paths.

British Mountaineering Council
http://www.thebmc.co.uk
Information on all matters of interest to mountaineers, including a searchable database of all climbing walls in the UK.

Countryside Commission
http://www.countrywalks.org.uk
Details and maps for 1,000 conservation walks in areas of open access throughout England. Searchable site.

Mountain huts in the Polish Tatry
http://www.cs.put.poznan.pl/holidays/tatry
Details of walks and huts in these lesser known mountains. Mostly in English.

Scottish Avalanche Information Service
http://www.sais.gov.uk
Excellent site giving up-to-date information on walking conditions in the Scottish Highlands (see Figure 9).

Wandelweb
http://macnet007.psy.uva.nl/users/Brand/Wandelen.html
Links to information on long distance trails.

Cycling
Bike Tours
http://www.cycling.uk.com/holidays
Offer a wide range of cycling holidays with backup services such as luggage transportation, a mechanic to deal with bike problems and, on larger tours, a nurse. Destination and tours include the Cotswolds, Cuba, Costa Rica, Portugal, Prague to Venice and an African cycling safari in Kenya.

Sustrans
http://www.sustrans.org.uk
A civil engineering charity which designs and builds routes for cyclists, walkers and people with disabilities. They are working on a 6,500-mile National Cycle Network for the United Kingdom. Details of existing and proposed routes on the site.

Travel with Bicycles
http://www.nicom.com/~georgef/access/index.html
An example of the web at its best. If you're planning to cycle or take your bike anywhere in the world look here first. It has all the information you'll ever need and some you never knew you needed. You can learn from others and share what you know (see Figure 10).

Other activities
Adult Residential Colleges Association (ARCA)
http://www.aredu.demon.co.uk
Offer a wide range of residential courses, covering most subjects. Examples include archaeology, fabric sculpture, garden design and wine appreciation. Colleges are often restored country houses,

beautifully situated and in their own grounds, the emphasis is on making learning a pleasurable experience. This site provides links to all ARCA colleges, many of which have online prospectuses and booking facilities. College brochures can be requested from ARCA's site and there is a subject index for all courses offered.

Association of British Travel Agents (ABTA)
http://www.abtanet.com
Travel agents who are members of the association are listed in various ways, one of the most useful being by holidays they specialise in. ABTA provide a message service which forwards your query by fax or e-mail to operators of interest to you.

British Adventure Holidays Association (BAHA)
http://www.baha.org.uk
Provides contact details for activity centres for children, families, adults, schools, groups and management training. Members of the BAHA have all agreed to abide by a code of practice and submit their centres to independent inspection.

British Trust for Conservation Volunteers
http://www.btcv.org.uk
Searchable database of conservation holidays in this country and abroad.

British Waterways
http://www.british-waterways.org
Information on Britain's canal system, including boating holidays, current navigation restrictions and waterways events. There is a

Claymoore Navigation	
Countrywide Cruisers	Shire Cruisers
Club Line Cruisers	Snaygill Boats
Gailey Marine	Viking Afloat

If you have chosen a canal please select it from the following list:

Canal [Llangollen Canal ▼]   Boat Type [Restaurant Boat ▼]

[List Boatyards]

Fig. 12. British Waterways search.

searchable database of companies in the United Kingdom offering holidays on cruisers, narrowboats and hotel boats.

Elderhostel
http://www.elderhostel.org
Provides educational adventures all over the world for those over 55. Tours include art and architecture study in Greece and field research in Belize on endangered dolphin populations.

Golf.com
http://www.golf.com
Everything there is to know about golf, including international course maps, publications and weather information.

Juggling Information Service
http://www.juggling.org
Learn to juggle on holiday or visit one of the many juggling festivals worldwide.

Museum Net
http://www.museums.co.uk
A searchable database of all UK museums. If you didn't know about the lawn mower or Postman Pat museum you can find it here, alongside all the more conventional ones. Excellent listings with links to individual museum web sites.

Ocean Youth Club UK
http://www.oyc.org.uk
An educational charity which promotes personal development through sailing and is open to all regardless of ability or circumstances. Offers 12 to 25 year olds the opportunity to learn to sail and take part in voyages, lasting from two to 20 days. No previous experience is needed and help with the cost is available through OYC's grant scheme and local fund-raising groups. Some voyages are open to older participants.

Surf Link
http://www.surflink.com
If you want to see what wave rather than web surfing has to offer this is the place to go. SurfCams show you just what you're missing whilst sitting at the computer; you can read, chat or watch surfing to your heart's content. The site also has a skateboarding section.

Travel World
http://travel.world.co.uk
An index of links to European travel agents and tour operators who provide specialist holidays, such as educational tours, sport related holidays, wildlife and safari holidays, citybreaks, cycling and sailing.

Working holidays

Camp Counselors USA
http://www.campcounselors.com
Camp America
http://www.aifs.org
Both provide the opportunity for those aged 18 and upwards to work in summer camps in America. The jobs last nine to eleven weeks, involve work with children and are mainly outdoors. You get your flight paid for and some pocket money, but there is a cost for registration and insurance.

Cool Works
http://www.coolworks.com
Provides details of jobs in 'Great Places'. Most of the work is seasonal. Information for non-US residents wanting to undertake temporary work in the US is included on the site (see Figure 13).

Council in Europe
http://www.ciee.org/europe/index.htm
Offers paid work experience, short-term jobs and exchange pro-grammes in a wide range of countries for students and recent graduates. Schemes include the Japan Exchange and Teaching programme (JET), and the US Internship scheme which allows some 4,000 students annually to work in the USA for six months.

International Student Travel Conference
http://www.istc.org/p_ho.asp
Promote and arrange work, study and travel exchange opportunities for students and other young people all over the world. Examples include working in a travel office in Jamaica, teaching arts and crafts in Paris, working for an airline in the US, doing layout for a weekly newspaper in Canada. There is an administration charge for participants.

Summer Jobs
http://www.summerjobs.com

Searchable, regularly updated database of jobs worldwide (see Figure 11). Their sister site **http://www.resortjobs.com** is also well worth a visit for details of seasonal work in holiday resorts.

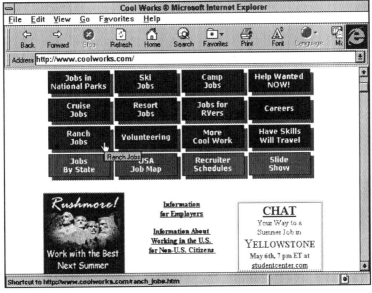

Fig. 13. Cool Works offers a world of possibilities.

4
Home Exchanging

WHAT IT MEANS

The basic idea of a home exchange is very simple. You exchange your home for someone else's for the duration of your holiday. It started in Europe about 40 years ago, with teachers in the Netherlands and Switzerland swapping homes for their summer holidays. From small beginnings it has grown into a thriving global activity. It is estimated that more than 60,000 travellers worldwide take exchange vacations each year. Exchanges cover most countries, all times of the year and can last from a weekend to a year.

Through a variety of means, thousands of people across the world make details of what they wish to swap available to others, exchanging homes, cars, camper vans, yachts and even children on a temporary basis.

People who have experienced home exchange are generally enthusiastic about the concept. It is not unusual to see them listed as having done over 20 exchanges. They have the opportunity to become part of a community in a way that other tourists don't and often develop long-term friendships with their exchange partners and new neighbours.

Any worries you have about lending your home are probably shared by your potential exchange partners. They are trusting you as much as you are them. Successful exchanges are the result of reciprocal honesty, care and trust.

Advantages of home exchanging

☑ You cut out the major cost of most holidays – accommodation.

☑ It gives you living space that is generally more roomy, well equipped and comfortable than any hotel.

☑ It offers a unique insight into living in a different country or even a different part of your own country.

☑ Exchange partners can help you sort out places to visit and things to do so that you make the best use of your holiday time.

☑ Your home, garden, pets and plants are looked after by your exchange partners.

☑ It's an opportunity to make new friendships.

☑ Exchange houses tend to be in more peaceful locations than most hotels, particularly in popular tourist locations – so you get the best of both worlds.

Disadvantages of home exchanging

☒ Your home and car are valuable assets, there is no guarantee that they will be cared for in the way that is acceptable to you.

☒ Getting ready takes a lot of time and effort.

☒ Your choice of destinations may be limited.

☒ It's addictive. Once you get used to the luxury of having a house/garden/pool all to yourself, it's hard to go back to paying for a small hotel room.

Other linked possibilities

Many agencies offer a lot more than house exchange: the following are common options.

House sitting

People who don't want to leave their home empty for long periods often look for others to care for it, their garden and possibly pets. Home exchange agencies can give members the opportunity to offer house sitting services or to request them.

Camper van exchange

Can be exchanged for another camper van or a house or boat. Useful when travelling a long distance.

Boat exchange

Often swapped for homes, camper vans or other boats, a quick way of getting to the bit of water you want to be on.

Hospitality exchange

What that means varies, and is up to individuals to arrange. Can be particularly appealing to single travellers.

Youth exchange

Send your children to stay with another family and then reciprocate at a later date. Good for improving language skills.

WHO IS HOME EXCHANGING FOR?

Home exchangers are people of all ages, from all occupational backgrounds in all parts of the world. You can find people with castles or cottages and everything in between. Most people feel comfortable when swapping their home for something of a comparable size and standard. Not everyone wants luxury, most people have ordinary comfortable homes and that is what they want to swap for.

Home exchange is particularly popular for:
● retired couples who now make up a substantial proportion of long-term travellers
● families with children looking for manageable and affordable holiday options
● single people of all ages, travelling alone.

Swapping like for like

Most exchange agencies reflect a mix in their listings but some specialist agencies only cater for certain groups, for example, the over 50s, Jewish home exchangers, or pilots (see Figure 14).

People tend to swap with those who have a similar family structure to their own because they often have the same accommodation needs and constraints, or lack of them on travel time. If you swap with someone whose children are a similar age to yours, you will automatically have the right equipment, toys, books and potential friends, and they will want school holiday times too.

ARRANGING AN EXCHANGE

In order to arrange an exchange you need to communicate what you have to offer to as large a group of potentially interested people as you can. Until recently, home exchanges were arranged through organisations which published and distributed directories listing details of members' homes and requirements.

Using an agency

Home exchange agencies typically have organisers in each country represented. They provide a framework for exchange by collecting the information, giving advice and dealing with queries. Members generally need to supply details three months before paper directory publication dates, and these details cannot be easily amended or

---

Welcome to the Seniors
Vacation and Home Exchange

The Only Exchange Exclusively For The Over 50 Age Group

**Not confined to Houses or Second Homes,
the Seniors Vacation and Home Exchange has been**
Expanded and *Now*
**allows you to exchange your
Motor Home or Caravan,
and to list
Bed and Breakfast Establishments
and Privately Owned Vacation Rental Properties**

A fair exchange is a good bargain!

Have you longed to visit faraway places, but just couldn't justify the cost? Maybe the Seniors Vacation and Home Exchange is the answer.

Many seniors around the country, or around the world share the same concerns about the high cost of vacations. Seniors Home Exchange can provide you with the very best alternative holiday at a cost that you never thought possible.

Fig. 14. Some agencies specialise in certain age groups.

updated. Organisations may publish several paper directories a year, usually between December and June.

Advantages of using an agency

☑ Using an established agency gives a feeling of security.

☑ Access to organisers with experience of all the aspects of home exchange.

☑ You know the person you are swapping with has registered with that agency.

☑ Guidelines and documentation to help you make an arrangement.

☑ Your privacy is protected as personal details are only made available to other members.

☑ It gives access to experienced home exchangers and thus to references from those they have exchanged with.

☑ Many organisations offer members specially negotiated insurance and travel deals tailored to the needs of the home exchanger.

☑ Agencies monitor what is going on and will exclude members about whom they receive complaints.

All agencies, however, clearly state that they take no responsibility for the outcomes of any arrangements made and that this is a private matter between individuals.

The Internet and home exchange agencies

The Internet has changed the way home exchange organisations work. Publishing, updating and sharing information is now significantly easier, cheaper and quicker. This represents a challenge to established agencies as it has led to an unprecedented growth in the number of organisations offering and individuals participating in home swapping.

Some established agencies have harnessed the potential of the Internet to offer a valuable extra facility to their members whilst continuing to offer them a paper-based directory. Experienced exchangers tend to remain loyal to the organisations they have used for many years, but there are signs that many are now making multiple registrations with Internet-based providers, or using newsgroups to reach a wide audience without intermediaries.

Advantages of web over paper directories

☑ Members can amend their entry at any time, so listings are always current.

☑ Well constructed databases make searching for suitable matches easier.

USA San Francisco Member no. 3600521

Exchange party: 2ad/2ch Max beds: 4 Occupation:

WHAT WE HAVE: located 20 minutes north of San Francisco's Golden Gate Bridge, in a beautiful private and family oriented community. We offer a 2 story large home that sits on private park with river to ocean and lagoons, 3 bedroom / 2 bath, comfortable, modern, well equipped with all amenities including cable TV, skylites, fireplace...etc, large kitchen, large deck, garden with trampoline, weekly maid. Car available (VW Jetta). The house is close to shopping and restaurants, 5 minutes drive to olympic size swimming pools, ocean beaches or sequoia woods are only 20 min drive away; 30 min to Napa & Sonoma wine country, 30 min to Berkeley, 4 hours to Yosemite National Park and Lake Tahoe, 3 hours from Monterey.

We are a professional couple with 2 kids of 8 and 12 years of age. Want 2-3 weeks in 2 different places, or 6-8 weeks in a grand place.

Desired destination: Europe (preferably (though not essential) near water and in or near a city.)

Dates and length of stay: 2-8 wks July & August

Fig. 15. A web home exchange listing from Haney's.

☑ Listings can be longer and more descriptive as space is not a problem.

☑ These organisations tend to be cheaper to join as they do not have printing and distribution costs.

☑ Potential exchange partners and organisers can be contacted by e-mail which is cheap, quick and effective.

☑ Many new organisations offer free membership to build up numbers.

Disadvantages of web-based listings

☒ Only those with Internet access can participate.

☒ Can lead to junk mail if your e-mail is made freely available to all the world. Some agencies offer password only access and/or an e-mail forwarding and filtering service.

☒ Some new web-based agencies are short lived.

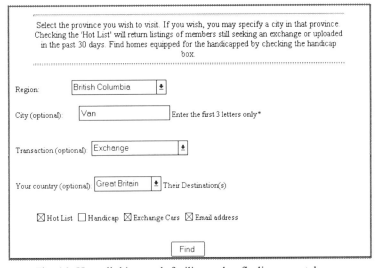

Fig. 16. Homelink's search facility makes finding a match easy.

Assessing new agencies

Because the Internet can allow unscrupulous people to offer what they can't deliver, it's important that you satisfy yourself that new, untried organisations will live up to the promises they make, particularly if you are paying a registration fee. Be wary of anything

There are 112 matching records. Displaying matches 1 through 50.

City	Dates	Destinations
Calgary, Alberta, 400k, NW	up to 7mo, July -->	AU GB O
Kelowna, 30k, N	4-5w, Apr-May Sep-Oct	GB Cornwall Devon+
Kelowna, 3m, S	3-4w, Jun or Sep	EUR GB M
Nanaimo	3-6w, May - Sep 98, *1999	GB C-Ottawa* USSW*
Nanaimo, 1k, E	Open, Open	I GB F
Nanaimo, 25k, N	3-4w, Jun - Sep	Scotland GB
Nanaimo, 25k, N	2w, Dec, Jul - Aug	A E F CH GB HI
Nanaimo, 45k, NW (Van Isl)	3w, March Sep & Oct	SA F G C IRL GB
Nanaimo - Vancouver Island	3-4w, Anytime	England GB
Nanaimo-Vancouver Island	4w, Aug - Sep	O GB* IRL F**
Vancouver	2-4w, Jan - Aug	D GB EUR
Vancouver	2-4w, May - Sep	F NL GB I IL G
Vancouver	2w, 1 - 31 May	GB F CH NL IRL +
Vancouver	2-4w, 15 Jun - 16 Aug	GB-Scot Eng IRL +
Vancouver	4-6w, Apr - Jun Sep - Nov	GB London

Fig. 17. The result of the search in Figure 16.

that seems too good to be true. Established organisations can appear more expensive, but they have a track record of delivering what they promise.

All agencies give access to glowing testimonials, but there is no way of knowing if these are fictional. The best way to check is to get in touch with people who have used them. If you have doubts about an organisation, post to a few travel related newsgroups asking for opinions on it. The majority in the cyber community wish to preserve the integrity of the Internet and are intolerant of charlatans. They will be quick to let you know of organisations and individuals who misuse it.

Things to check

- How long the organisation has been established. If it's been around a few years that's some safeguard, but everyone has to start some time.

- Some organisations publish a code of practice. Although this does not guarantee anything, it shows they've thought about the issues.

- Avoid agencies that don't have an 'about us' section or contact details other than e-mail.

Using the Internet for exchange without an agency

The Internet with its ease of communication makes it possible to show the world what you have to offer. You can arrange a home exchange without an intermediary by using newsgroups, bulletin boards and mailing lists.

These could be travel-related resources, professional groups or ones that cover a subject you're interested in. If you're a passionate bird-watcher in Britain you may find a potential home exchange to Sweden through a birdwatching rather than a travel newsgroup. If you're concerned about the ecological impact of tourism, you may be interested in subscribing to a mailing list such as Green Travel and posting details of what you have to offer. Exchange is an ecologically friendly form of tourism, you make very little impact on the environment by using someone else's home. For information on using newsgroups and mailing lists see Chapter 9.

Some web sites that deal with travel such as Frommers and Lonely Planet incorporate bulletin boards or newsgroups where you can post offers of hospitality or home exchange.

If you are doing a home exchange without an intermediary you need to take the same precautions and ask for the same information as you would with an agency. There is no one to complain to if things don't work out, but an agency can't really do more than listen to your complaint.

INTERNET TECHNIQUES FOR HOME EXCHANGERS

Enhancing your listing, researching your offers

Whichever method you use to look for an exchange, the Internet provides additional resources to make your offer more attractive and your research more effective. It's a good idea to include details of web sites that cover your area. These can include tourist information, local papers, videos, web cameras, maps, and weather details. It saves you a lot on postage and enables your partners to have a good look at the area. You should ask your partners for details of similar resources covering their locality, to help with your decision-making.

It's not difficult to make your own web site, most Internet Service Providers give you space for this. Many exchangers use it to provide detailed information and pictures about themselves, their home and surroundings, and to incorporate relevant links. Anyone using a search engine to look for sites on home exchange would then find your site, or it could be used as a reference source for people who had found your details through an agency or newsgroup.

Children all over the world increasingly have access to the Internet at school. Many schools in the UK and elsewhere have created sites that reflect their surroundings. These are used to encourage communication between children in different countries. In the near future children in the UK will be given e-mail addresses and web space. Parents can capitalise on this and use it to involve children in holiday planning.

Using e-mail for home exchange

Your first contact with potential partners is important, you need to engage their interest and establish a dialogue. Speed of communication exchange is important, so e-mail is an excellent tool to use. Initially you should:

- Send a brief introductory note about your family and home. Include the details in the main body rather than sending an attachment.

- Personalise your message where possible by adding something that shows you have looked seriously at their entry.

- If you do send copies, use the 'blind copy' facility.

- Ask for a reply even if it is negative. It helps you keep track of what is happening.

- Ask if they would like to receive pictures and what file attachments their software can cope with.

Once you have interest in your offer, e-mail is an ideal way to keep in touch. It eliminates weeks of delay between sending letters and waiting for replies.

Avoiding junk mail

Placing your details on a public site such as ETN or posting details to a newsgroup can lead to junk mail. This nuisance can be minimised by setting up a specific e-mail address for exchange purposes – most providers offer more than one e-mail address. It is also possible to set up free web-based e-mail or forwarding accounts for this purpose. If you find you are getting junk mail you can change that address.

If you are new to using e-mail there is a brief guide for beginners in Chapter 9.

QUESTIONS AND ANSWERS

Is my home good enough?
This appears to be the most common worry amongst home exchangers. Standards of accommodation vary. It is often difficult for someone in the UK to match the number of bathrooms of the average US house for example. Most people who exchange don't want a replica of their own home and relish differences. What is important is that the home should be clean and comfortable. The preliminary stages of an arrangement are devoted to description and exploration of what is on offer. It is important to be honest and, if you are aware of obvious discrepancies between homes, to raise that matter with your potential partners. The type of people who want to exchange are usually flexible and can live without their hot tub, pool, maid, dishwasher, video or air conditioning for a few weeks. What is essential is that they have an accurate description on which to base their decision to exchange.

Is their home good enough?
It's up to you to find out. Ask for internal and external pictures. If they have done an exchange before ask for references. If you have very exacting standards for your holiday accommodation then home exchange may not be for you, it requires some flexibility.

Will they look after my things?
Most exchangers report having found their home cleaner than when they left it. People involved in home exchange are unanimous in saying they take more care of other people's possessions than they do of their own. Of course standards of care and cleanliness can vary. It's a good idea to make clear what your expectations are and get partners to agree. If you have particularly valuable or delicate items, put them away.

What if I break something of theirs?
No matter how careful you are, accidents can happen. It is accepted practice to replace anything you are responsible for breaking. When you arrive in your holiday home take time to move things that look fragile or expensive out of harm's way. Remember to put them back when you leave!

How can I check what the neighbourhood is like?
Ask your exchangees, they will tell you whether it's lively or quiet.

However, when people have lived in a place for some time they stop noticing things that can be a nuisance to others such as road or rail noise. Ask for street maps or get them off the web, communicate with others who have been there, read electronic editions of the local paper.

What if they smoke or leave me with a huge phone or electricity bill?
All these things should be discussed and agreed on before making a commitment to exchange. Most exchange registration forms ask people to state whether they want smokers in their house. It is normal for individuals to pay the utility bills for their own home as they are likely to use roughly the same amount of power and water in their partner's home. The cost of phone calls, however, is generally covered by the person making the calls. Home exchangers tend to be reasonable, honest people. A little planning and effective communication can avoid a lot of potential problems. Discuss your concerns fully before making an agreement.

CASE STUDIES

Tom's suggestion is not well received
One of Tom's colleagues has a solicitor from Thailand staying with him and is planning to pay a return visit later in the year. He has arranged this through an organisation that promotes hospitality exchanges. Tom discusses the idea with Lorna and they look at the Servas web site. Lorna is quite keen, but the children are adamant that they would not enjoy staying with another family. Their parents reluctantly concede that it would not be fair to impose their children on anyone else and decide to postpone such a venture until the children leave home. Tom decides to research summer camps for children . . .

Mary uses e-mail to arrange a home exchange
Mary's group have been making contact with similar training courses around the country, as a way of trying out e-mail. Mary chooses to write to parents on an IT course at a school in York. When she mentions that she is planning a holiday there with her children, Rhona, one of the York course participants, suggests a house swap. She wants to take her children to London over half term. At first Mary is worried that her house is not good enough, but Rhona talks her round. She convinces Mary that the sort of house she stays in does not matter to her. She wants somewhere quiet, roomy and with things for the children to do.

Chris helps his parents and himself

Chris's parents are looking at the idea of a long term home exchange. They have decided this will suit them better than a hospitality swap. It also suits Chris. The organisation that interests them, Seniors, has lots of members in parts of the US that he would like to visit too. He sees a possible cheap accommodation option for himself if he can fix up an internship in the same area.

SITESEEING TIPS

The following is a selection of web sites that deal with home and hospitality exchange. They have been chosen to show the variety of what is available. This is a dynamic and growing area on the web with new organisations springing up, and some closing down. You can find more by using a search engine or directory.

European Travel Network
http://www.etn.nl/fullindex.htm
This Dutch site offers everything travellers need, including a free facility for listing homes for exchange or rent. That list is relatively short, but is frequently updated. ETN also offers links to discount airfares, hotels and cruises from consolidators, travel agents, bucket shops and tour operators in 144 countries. There are also links to newsgroups and other travel related sites.

Frommers
http://www.frommers.com
The Travel Message Board section gives the opportunity to arrange hospitality exchanges. 'Hospitality' is defined by the person offering. It could be meeting someone for a drink, showing them round local attractions or offering free accommodation in return for the same later.

Haney's Home Exchange
http://www.sima.dk/haneys
Danish home exchange club which was established over 20 years ago. It is free to join, you only pay (currently $80) when you arrange an exchange. There is a database of members you can search, or you can submit your details for custom matching. Lots of Danish and North European participants but many other countries represented too. Haney's have had an Internet presence for the last three years and this has led to marked increase in membership.

Holi Swaps
http://www.holi-swaps.com
New UK-based agency costing $30 a year. Members receive a free
e-mail newsletter that keeps them abreast of latest developments. The
site has many useful links and features including a tutorial you can
download. This allows you to browse offline through selected pages
from their site to see how it works without running up phone bills.

HomeExchange.COM
http://www.homeexchange.com/index.htm
US-based agency which offers exchanges in 30 countries. The database can be read in German, Spanish, French, Italian and English.
Current fee for membership is $30; a newsletter is available for an
extra subscription.

Homelink International
http://www.swapnow.com
One of the original home exchange organisations, it was established
in 1952 and now has registered offices in 30 countries with over 11,500
listings. Membership costs £80 a year which entitles you to five paper
directories and a listing on their web site. This well established and
respected organisation has made excellent use of the Internet. Its
easy-to-search database can be viewed in English, German, Dutch,
French or Spanish. Members who are still looking can put themselves
on a hot list for a month at a time so it's possible to just search current
listings. The UK organisers are extremely helpful and can be
contacted by e-mail or more traditional means. UK members with
e-mail addresses are given a Homelink address which filters and
forwards their e-mail thus preventing junk mailers having access to
personal e-mail addresses.

Latitudes Home Exchange
http://www.iinet.net.au/~homeswap
Latitudes, established in 1993, offer a range of exchange homes in
over 30 countries, but say they are 'small enough to remember your
name'. They offer a 'custom matching service' which introduces
members with matching criteria to each other, as well as a traditional
'find your own' directory service. Directory membership is £50,
custom matching is £150. Head office is in Perth, Australia, with
branch offices in the UK, South Africa, New Zealand, the Middle
East and USA.

Réseau international d'échange de foyers
http://www.cyberlab.ch/exchange
Swiss-based home exchange and vacation rental organisation. All listings are Internet based. Site can be viewed in English, French, Spanish and German. Membership starts at $39 a year. Free services include a travel companion search, mailing list membership, access to discussion forum on related issues, all listings of one country or one US state by e-mail, and access to rental listings.

Seniors Vacation and Home Exchange
http://www.seniorshomeexchange.com
An agency catering exclusively for the over 50s. It's based in Canada but covers over 20 countries. Membership is $20 for two years. All listings have e-mail addresses. There is a selection of bed and breakfast and rental listings too (see Figure 14).

Servas
http://www.servas.org
An international network of 'hosts and travellers building peace and inter-cultural understanding'. Membership costs $65 a year. Prospective members have to write a letter of introduction and are interviewed by an existing member.

Stayfree Holiday Club
http://www.stayfree.org
Offer homes for exchange in 25 countries, including some not often found in exchange databases such as Macedonia and South Korea. It is an organisation dedicated to promoting peace and understanding between people of different cultures and see home exchange as promoting this. There is an annual membership fee of $49. Stayfree plan to donate a percentage of profits to charities of the members' choice.

Vacation Homes Unlimited
http://www.vacation-homes.com
Offer exchange opportunities in over 40 countries, with most listings for US, UK, Canada, Australia, New Zealand and the Caribbean. They have a directory and Internet option and a range of membership fees for different services, starting at $65 a year. The searchable database is quick and easy to use.

5
Getting There

Travellers fall into two categories: those who want to get there as quickly as possible and those for whom the journey is an enjoyable part of the holiday. Whichever you are and whatever form of transport you are using the Internet will help you plan and give you access to details of discounts and special offers. Because transport information changes quickly, the Internet is the ideal medium for getting details which are accurate and up to date, so helping make your journey as trouble free as possible.

GOING BY CAR

You can use web-based information to:

- work out the best routes
- check distances
- obtain maps and driving directions
- check current traffic conditions, often via live cameras
- participate in ride sharing
- check details of major roadworks and other disruptions
- check the cost of tolls and other road charges
- find details of traffic regulations and equipment needed in the countries you will be visiting
- compare petrol prices
- obtain information on secure parking.

Journey planners
A large number of sites offer free journey planning facilities. The map sites listed in Chapter 7 offer detailed maps and driving directions between any addresses in the USA. European sites are beginning to

The route planner is also available in other languages:

[English ▼] [Switch]

Please enter your departure and destination locations and add via locations, if any:

Departure [London]   Via

Arrival [Geneva]   [   ] [   ]

Route description: **Criterium:**   **Means of transport:**

◉ Normal route description   ◉ Fastest   ◉ Car
○ Detailed route description   ○ Shortest   ○ Truck

euroShell will show you the route! [Calculate Route]

The euroShell Route Planner can also calculate an extensive route, including costs and travel time.

Fig. 18. euroShell's free journey planner.

offer similar services, but these tend to be between major cities rather than specific streets. Shell, for example provide a free service that produces maps and written directions for journeys between major centres in Europe. It also calculates the time and cost of the trip.

Checking for delays

The main providers of information on roadworks, expected delays and other matters of interest to the motorist are motoring organisations such as the AA and the RAC. Their web sites have extensive, up to the minute information on road conditions in this country and abroad, plus an impressive range of related information including comparative petrol costs and details of secure car parks. Most

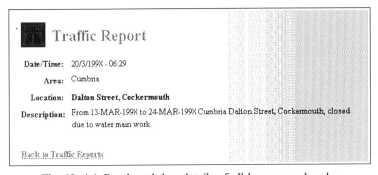

Fig. 19. AA Roadwatch has details of all known roadworks.

national motoring organisations have web sites, normally only in the language of their country. A selection is listed at the end of this chapter, others can be found using a search engine or directory.

Some government transport departments provide information to help motorists, including live traffic maps, cameras, detailed motoring and traffic information.

Car hire

Using the web can be a quick and effective way to compare car hire rates and find special offers. Travelocity offer the facility to compare rates amongst several of the large companies. However, you can also use the web to search for smaller local companies which may be cheaper. It can be worth looking at the local offices of multinational car hire companies as they do charge different rates in different countries. You can use your credit card to pay in the local currency. As *Yellow Pages* and business directories for most countries are now available on the web, it's easy to find details of companies that do not have a web presence and contact them by more conventional means.

Airlines often have cheap car hire deals: American Airlines, for example, have offers from airports in the US posted in their electronic newsletter (see Chapter 9). When making comparisons check:

- local taxes and VAT
- extra insurance premiums
- charges for other drivers
- age restrictions
- mileage charges
- after hours pick-up/delivery charges.

Ask for a written quotation via e-mail to confirm the total price and pick-up arrangements. This gives you much more security than a telephone booking. Once car hire companies have your credit card details they can impose extra charges which they claim to have told you about. It's easier to prove what was agreed at the time of booking if you have written confirmation.

Ride sharing

There are lots of ways to travel by car even if you don't own or don't want to hire one. The UK is one of the most difficult European countries in which to arrange this formally, but there are some web sites that match people wanting a lift to those offering one.

In mainland Europe well established schemes are used by travellers for all sorts of journeys. In Germany Mitfahrzentralen arranges over 1.5 million lifts a year. Other large European schemes are Autostop in France and Taxistop in Belgium. They have offices in most major cities and exploit the cheap, easy communication that the web offers. There is usually a registration fee and passengers make their own arrangements for sharing petrol costs with drivers.

Hitchhiking

Hitchhiking is less safe and less certain than ride sharing, but if that appeals to you, then you can read about the experiences and suggestions of others in great detail on the Internet. There are sites and newsgroups devoted to this topic with hints on techniques, best places and safety. Green Travel, listed at the end of this chapter, has a excellent page of links for hitchhikers.

Driveaways

This inexpensive way of getting the use of a car is common in North America. You perform a service for someone who wants their car in another part of the continent but does not have time to drive it there. This is normally done through a driveaway company which acts as an intermediary. The main features are:

- Driveaways are usually for long distances, *eg* Ottawa to Florida.

- You are given a certain time to complete the journey, for example New York to Los Angeles in 8 days. This can be extended for a fee.

- Some companies give a petrol allowance, but it's not common, you normally pay for your own.

- You pay all your own accommodation expenses.

- You pay a deposit, ranging from $300 to $500 depending on your age. This is refunded when the car is delivered in good condition.

- There are age restrictions – you usually need to be over 21.

- Some companies charge an administration fee.

- The company normally pays for car insurance, but not medical or travel insurance.

- You may be required to clean the car before it is returned to the owner.

GOING BY BUS

Buses are still a cheap form of public transport. A ban on smoking and the introduction of couchette facilities have made long journeys more comfortable. Buses often go to places where trains don't and where you may not wish to take your car.

Countries with integrated public transport systems may offer passes covering all their forms of transport. The Swiss Railcard, for example, allows unlimited use of trains, buses, boats and some cable cars. Bus companies use the web to show details of timetables, special offers, tours and related information.

GOING BY PLANE

You can use the Internet to find information on all aspects of air travel, from safety issues to arrival times, and of course the best priced tickets to everywhere in the world. There are web sites, mailing lists and newsgroups on all aspects of air travel.

Air fare search agents

Many travel related web sites offer a customised 'agent' which searches the world's computer reservation systems for the best fares to chosen destinations. These are usually owned by airlines. One of the best known is Travelocity (owned by American Airlines) but several others perform a similar function. They have the following features:

- e-mail alerts to keep you up to date with fare bargains and price changes

- links to related information and offers such as hotels and car hire

- online reservation and booking

- promotions and special offers such as extra frequent flyer miles or seat auctions.

These sites are for scheduled rather than charter flights and many of the low cost airlines, like Easy Jet **(http://www.easyjet.com)** do not participate in them. In order to get the best fare offers you need to compare what you find here with information both on and off the Internet.

An interesting new service is offered by the US company Priceline which allows buyers of airline tickets to name the price they're willing to pay. Airlines then look at these offers and decide if they will accept them. It's estimated that there are 500,000 empty seats on domestic and international flights from the US every day and this is an innovative way of filling them.

Getting the best priced air tickets

Official fares between most countries are set by IATA, so most computer systems list only IATA fares for international flights. It's easy to find entirely legal 'consolidator' tickets sold for considerably less than the official price. To get the best fare bargains you should:

- ☑ Register with several fare finder sites to get an idea of price range.
- ☑ Subscribe to airline and fare finder newsletters.
- ☑ Look at the web sites of airlines matched by your fare finder to see if they have special offers for direct online booking.
- ☑ Use Teletext and the weekend papers to check which low cost and charter airlines fly the route you want. If they have a web site check for offers.
- ☑ Do the same for 'bucket shops' and travel agents advertising on Teletext and in the papers. They often buy up left over charter tickets.
- ☑ Use on and offline travel agents. They can sometimes get a better price.

Airlines

Most airlines now have a web site. At their simplest these offer details of schedules and fares. A small but growing number have online booking and e-ticketing facilities. These sometimes include a discount or boost in air miles for online bookers. As some UK travel agents are imposing surcharges on transactions under £75, the opportunity to book directly with an airline for low cost seats can represent a valuable saving. The most extensive and sophisticated sites are those serving the American market but European carriers are increasingly using the potential of the Internet.

Many North American carriers have special web-only offers and seat auctions for flights originating in the US or Canada. These are often, but not always, for last minute departures, a sort of standby without the standing (see Figure 20). Several offer e-mail newsletters or notifications of current cheap deals that can include car hire and accommodation as well as flights. Their European offices and European airlines themselves are reluctant to follow suit. There seems to be a feeling that as fewer people use the Internet in Europe, it would discriminate against those without access, but that situation is likely to change.

America West puts the US and Vancouver on sale
America West is offering some great fares this week for travel in the US and to Vancouver. Fares start at $34 each way, while transcontinental flights start at $119 each way (taxes not included). The travel dates on sale are April 14 through September 30. To qualify for these fares, a minimum stay of at least one Saturday night is required. The lowest fares are available during what the airline considers 'off-peak' times: after noon on Mondays through 11:59 a.m on Thursdays and all day Saturday (fares at other times are higher). Your tickets must be purchased within 24 hours after making reservations and are non-refundable. The fares apply to round-trip travel only. There are no black-out dates, but tickets are only on sale until this Friday, March 20, so you'll need to act fast.

Fig. 20. Cheap web offers may exclude taxes and other charges.

Keeping up to date with offers via e-mail
Several airlines operate e-mail lists that keep you updated on special fares and other deals. These are mainly for trips originating in North America. Gateway travel sites often link to subscription pages. The Epicurious site, for example, enables you to subscribe to the newsletters of five American carriers.

E-ticketing
This relatively new facility is offered by a number of airlines. Passengers who book online get an ID number instead of a ticket. However, as many airlines then send an itinerary and a passenger receipt by traditional mail, you've still got something to lose or leave at home!

GOING BY TRAIN

Rail companies have made good use of the web and most national railway networks have web sites, with all the information you need and online booking facilities. The countries which have efficient rail networks mirror that with efficient web sites. Swiss Railways, for

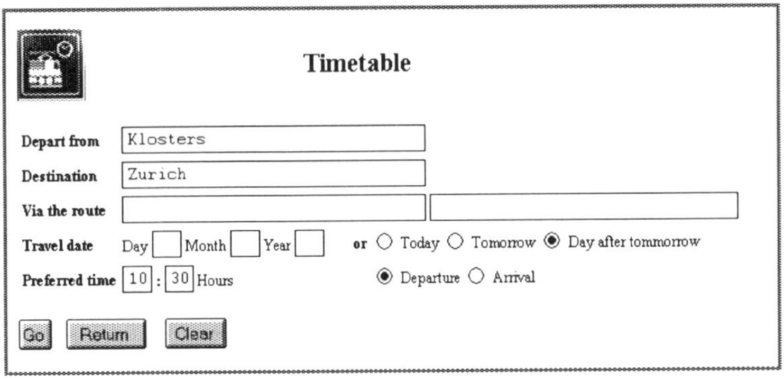

Fig. 21. The Swiss rail search page.

example, have a searchable site where you can quickly find and book what you need (see Figure 21). They also include details of their passes and special offers. The most difficult rail system to understand is probably in the UK, as there is no national rail network, but a fragmented collection of companies.

The web is also a good place to find details of many of the special narrow gauge lines and steam trains such as Cumbria's La'al Ratty (http://www.ravenglass-railway.co.uk). Several travel sites and some national railway sites provide links to railways worldwide. Details of some of the more exotic and unusual routes are often maintained by individuals with an interest in a particular region or in rail travel. For example, timetables for the Trans Mongolian, Trans Siberian and Trans Manchurian railways can be accessed from a server at an Australian university. Numerous newsgroups are related to train travel discussions and it is easy to get advice and details of others' experiences. These range from discussions on the length of some UK commuter journeys to more esoteric topics (see Figure 22).

Underground rail systems

Most of the world's large cities have underground systems that provide cheap and efficient transport but can be daunting to those not familiar with them. Their web sites with detailed maps and related information make it possible to familiarise yourself before you go. Some such as the Moscow Underground site (http://www.metro.ru) are in the language of their country. If you have trouble understanding the site you'll probably have similar trouble navigating the system.

A good starting point is the excellent Subway Navigator site available in English and French (see Figure 23). It aims to provide

Tips for travel by train in Russia

1. Learn to read the Cyrillic alphabet, this will assist you with reading signs and communicating with people.

2. Dress modestly, wear clothes like the locals around you. If you flaunt wealth then you'll become a target for thieves.

3. Carry some food on the train, don't rely on the dining car. It usually serves a limited menu as most menu items will not be available (example menu: goulash and borsch), it is also not particularly cheap. Food such as potatoes and eggs is available at station platforms often from elderly women. From China a supply of instant noodles is useful.

4. Carry a supply of toilet paper, it may also be bought at stations but often not.

5. Always double check departure times at stations en route or you'll get left behind; sometimes there is little warning that trains are departing (apart from a rush of traders heading for the nearest door).

6. Take some reading material, but not too much, you will want to see the countryside and enjoy the company on the train.

7. Take care with valuables, backpacks can be put in a box under the lower seats, or else it is good to sleep on them.

8. If you meet Russians, be prepared to drink half a bottle of vodka; they generally take three glasses each, so it is OK to ask them to put only a little (Russian: *malo*) in each glass.

Fig. 22. Train travellers can benefit from practical advice in newsgroups.

links to all the world's underground systems and gives detailed travel directions. As it is maintained by an individual it does get out of date, so it is worth visiting official sites too.

GOING BY BOAT

The Channel Tunnel has resulted in cheaper ferry fares to France and Belgium from the UK. All the companies are competing to attract customers and most advertise offers on the web. Several sites take the hard work out of finding specific operators, notably Seaview and A2B, by offering an index to all sailings from the UK. There are also links to information on cruises and passages on working ships.

If you're looking for a cheap alternative to cruising, investigate crewing agencies. There are several on the web which for a small fee

Route from 'Bethnal Green' to 'Embankment' in the London subway.

Result of the route search from 'Bethnal Green' to 'Embankment'.

Estimated time = 25 minutes

- Line 'Central', Direction 'Ealing Broadway' or 'West Ruislip'
  - □ Bethnal Green
  - □ Liverpool Street
  - □ Bank
- Line 'Circle', Direction 'Baker Street'
  - □ Monument
  - □ Cannon Street
  - □ Mansion House
  - □ Blackfriars
  - □ Temple
  - □ Embankment

Sorry, you can't display the graphical map. It is not available for your town. However, you can do something to remedy this situation.

You can also search a route in another city, get further information about the subway navigator and you can even send a message to the author.

Fig. 23. The Subway Navigator plans the route for you.

will help match you up with some wonderful sounding trips. Alternatively you could search through postings in related newsgroups for free.

Every country with a coastline has companies offering transport by sea and many shipping companies have details on the web. These can most easily be found using a country specific search engine with keywords such as ferries/sailings/ships.

Some ferry operators offer surprising additional services that can add interest to your journey, the Nootka Sound Service of British Columbian Ferries (http://www.island.net/~mvuchuck), for example, provides transportation for canoeists and arranges launches for them en route!

CASE STUDIES

Mary's class plan a day trip

Mary's friend Sue has been doing her Internet research project on shopping in Calais. Using information from http://www.seaview.co.uk she persuades the rest of them that it's worth taking one of the day trip offers to go shopping. The three with the biggest car boots are nominated as drivers. Mary helps Sue put together a folder of maps, shop opening hours and details of things other than drink that are worth going to France for.

Chris learns something new about his father

Chris's parents are in the final stages of arranging a home exchange to San Francisco. He is a little confused when they ask him to find prices for flights to Florida. His father owns up to wanting to relive something he did when he was 20, a driveaway across America. Chris is fascinated, he can't remember his father ever mentioning a trip to America and driveaway means nothing to him. He uses the web to search for cheap flights and decides to see what he can find on driveaways, although his dad has already contacted the company he used before. What he discovers opens up all sorts of new possibilities and Chris begins to rethink his own travel plans.

Tom finds peace of mind

Tom's work takes him to different places around the country. He dislikes leaving his car in anonymous multi storey car parks, where he never feels it's quite safe. While looking at breakdown insurance details for his ski trip he comes across the secure car parks listing on the AA web site.

SITESEEING TIPS

General

Directory of Transportation Resources
http://dragon.princeton.edu/~dhb
A comprehensive collection of links to transport related sites everywhere. You can find information on just about every transport system in the world here.

TravelShop
http://www.travelshop.de/english.htm
Takes you to the English version of this German site. A treasure trove of travel links including a listing of links to all airlines and national railways with web sites.

Driving information

The AA
http://www.theaa.co.uk
Current information on UK and European traffic conditions. There is lots of related travel and motoring information including lists of secure car parks in the UK (see Figure 24).

Fuel price report

Quoted in sterling equivalent and local currency.

Country	Local Currency Litre			Sterling Litre		
	Leaded	Unleaded	Diesel	Leaded	Unleaded	Diesel
Austria (Schillings)	-	11.90	9.45	-	58.85	46.74
Belgium (B/Francs)	40.40	37.20	28.10	68.04	62.65	47.32
Bulgaria (leva) *	1140.00	1070.00	630.00	-	-	-
Croatia (HRD) *	4.00	3.80	3.40	-	-	-
Czech Rep. (Koruna)	23.20	23.00	19.30	44.72	44.33	37.20
Denmark (Krona)	6.73	6.56	5.31	60.96	59.42	48.10
Finland (Markka)	-	5.69	3.85	-	64.73	43.80
France (Francs)	6.44	6.20	4.43	66.69	64.20	45.87
Germany (D/M)	-	1.65	1.21	-	57.07	41.85
Greece (Drach.)	241.00	227.00	172.00	52.77	49.71	37.66
Holland (Guilders)	-	2.14	1.48	-	65.99	45.64
Hungary (HUF)	150.40	143.40	134.90	49.95	47.63	44.80
Ireland (Pt)	0.70	0.65	0.64	61.24	56.87	55.99

Fig. 24. The AA's site compares fuel costs across Europe.

Other motoring organisations:

Australia **http://www.aaa.asn.au**
Germany **http://www.adac.de**
Spain **http://www.aseta.es**
America **http://www.aaa.com**
Canada **http://www.caa.ca**

euroShell Route Planner
http://www.euroshell.com
Excellent site that works out the shortest or fastest journey between main centres in Europe. All Shell petrol stations on the route are highlighted and can be 'visited' to check services offered and opening times.

French Ministry of Transport
http://www.equipement.gouv.fr/bisonfute/index.htm
The above URL takes you to the *Bison Futé* pages. This is a route system which aims to ease traffic congestion at peak holiday times in France.

RAC
http://www.rac.co.uk
Live traffic information for the UK and accommodation and journey planners.

Spanish Ministry of the Interior
http://www.dgt.es/ingles/iindex.html
Has 'live' maps with details of current traffic flow, information on road conditions, motorway tolls, restrictions and likely hold-ups, new roads, traffic legislation and safety rules and advice for drivers in Spain. There is an English version of the index page, but the rest of the site is in Spanish.

Driveaways, ride sharing and hitchhiking

Auto Driveaway Co
http://www.angelfire.com/biz/driveaway
Based in Washington DC. Gives details of cars currently available for driveaways.

Toronto Driveaway
http://www.torontodriveaway.com
Established Canadian company. Specialise in 'snowbird' deliveries between Toronto and Florida. They reimburse petrol and return air fare costs. Online application form.

Green Travel – hitchhikers' links
http://www.green-travel.com/hitch.htm
This page has an excellent set of links to sites providing information on driveaway, ride sharing, hitchhiking and related guidebooks.

Sites that put travellers in touch with drivers offering lifts include:
Belgium – Taxistop
http://www.taxistop.be

France – Les services du Gnafou
http://astop.remcomp.fr

Germany – Mitfahrzentrale
http://www.uni-stuttgart.de/Mfg/mfg.html

Italy – Autostop
http://www.topnet.it/seblie/autostop.html

Sweden – Liftarens
http://www.torget.se/liftaren

Buses
Greyhound (US)
http://www.greyhound.com
Details of fares, schedules, special offers, discounts, passes and lots of related links.

National Express (UK)
http://www.nationalexpress.co.uk
Detailed information on timetables, fares, discount offers, airport and European services.

Air travel information
Good places to get independent overviews of all matters related to the Internet and air fares are:

Airline FAQs
http://iecc.com/airline/airinfo.html
This URL takes you to a list maintained by John Levine as a hobby. Not to be missed if you are going to use the web for buying air travel. Though the information is primarily on journeys originating in the US, he offers insights into European providers, from British Airways to Manx Airlines. As European carriers make greater use of the web the information becomes applicable to all travellers. There are details of travel agents on the web who offer air ticket deals, with a subsection for the 'not recommended'.

You can also get this list by e-mail every Sunday by sending a message containing the line 'subscribe airline' to **majordomo@iecc. com**.

Air traveller's handbook
http://www.cs.cmu.edu/afs/cs/user/mkant/Public/Trave/airfare.htm
The Air Traveller's Handbook is the FAQ posting for the rec.travel. air newsgroup. It includes a comprehensive annotated collection of links to air and general travel resources on the Internet with an emphasis on obtaining cheap fares, although other topics are covered. US orientated but useful for all.

Travel agents and fare searchers

The following is a small selection of travel agents making use of the web to sell discounted air tickets. The number available on the web grows daily and can be accessed via search directories such as Yahoo in Business and Economy: Companies: Travel: Airlines: Online Reservations section or by searching using key words such as **travel agents, tour operators, air fares**. *Only use agencies that show evidence of financial bonding (see Chapter 2).*

Destinations
http://www.destinations.co.uk

Fare Busters
http://www.farebusters.com

Flight Line
http://www.flightline.co.uk

The Travel Bug
http://www.travel-bug.co.uk

FLIFO
http://www.flifo.com
Offers online search and booking for flights, car hire and hotels. A 'fare buster' feature looks for cheaper flights close to the ones you asked for. Option of contacting a Flifo operator by phone (in the US) to complete your booking offline if you are not happy with online booking.

Priceline
http://www.priceline.com
Invites you to submit details of where you want to depart from and go to, travel dates and what you're willing to pay. Your request is passed on to airlines with empty seats and you are e-mailed with details of whether your 'bid' has been accepted. Replies are available within one hour for US domestic flights and 24 hours for international travel. Currently, all travel must originate within the 50 United States or Puerto Rico. They plan to add 'foreign' originating travel in the near future.

Travel Epicurious

http://travel.epicurious.com/travel/c_planning/02_airfares/intro.html
This page contains a good overview of how to get bargain airfares
and makes signing up for airline newsletters easy.

Travelocity

http://www.travelocity.com
American Airline's Travelocity is one of the largest fare search sites
and many providers of travel information link to it. Once you have
registered your search with them you will be notified of price changes
by e-mail. If you have a pager, Travelocity will keep you updated with
details of changes or delays to your flight. This site also provides
access to related information and offers such as accommodation and
car hire.

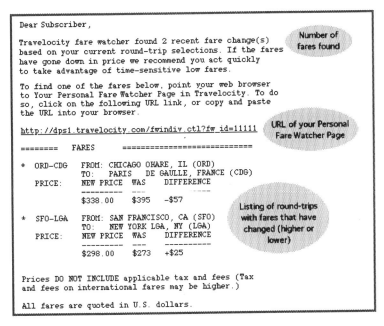

Fig. 25. Sample Travelocity e-mail.

Airlines
Infotec Travel
http://www.infotec-travel.com
Links to all airlines and airports in the world with web sites.

The following airlines offered online booking at the time of writing All these systems require secure servers (see Chapter 2).

Air Canada
http://w3.aircanada.ca

Alaska Airlines
http://www.alaskaair.com

America West Airlines
http://www.americawest.com

American Airlines
http://www.americanair.com

British Airways
http://www.british-airways.com

British Midland
http://www.iflybritishmidland.com

Continental Airlines
http://www.flycontinental.com

Delta Airlines
http://www.delta-air.com

Lufthansa Airlines
http://www.lufthansa.co.uk
http://www.lufthansa.com

Northwest Airlines
http://www.nwa.com

KLM
http://www.klmuk.com

Southwest Airlines
http://www.swavacations.com

TWA
http://www.twa.com

Virgin Atlantic
http://www.ezbook virgin.com

Railways

The European Railway Server
http://mercurio.iet.unipi.it/hometxt.html
Provides information about the European railways, for rail enthusiasts

as well as travellers, with links to experts in other countries, sites with timetables and unofficial sites.

Swiss Railways
http://www.rail.ch

German railways
http://www.bahn.de
These sites, available in English and German, are as efficient as the rail systems. Searchable timetable and connection information, online booking, details of special offers and useful related links.

UK Railways on the Net
http://www.rail.co.uk
A brave effort to make sense of the new fragmented and confused system. There is a travel planner, an index of train operating companies, weekend travel news and route maps.

Timetable information is provided by a link to Railtrack which can be accessed separately at **http://www.railtrack.co.uk** where you can find the phone numbers for companies that accept telephone bookings. Interestingly there is a toll free number for US callers but UK customers have to pay for their calls.

The Subway Navigator
http://metro.jussieu.fr:10001
Details of undergrounds for most cities in the world, from the Tyneside Metro to Caracas. Maps and details of nearby attractions are available for some.

Ships
A2B Travel. (British Ferry Schedules and Services)
http://www.a2btravel.com/ferry.html
Over 80 ferry timetables for departures to and from the UK. You can also investigate car hire, coach and rail journeys.

Crewseekers International
http://www.crewseekers.co.uk
Finds work for amateur crews. Registration is for a fee.

SeaView Cruise and Ferry Information Service
http://www.seaview.co.uk
Comprehensive information for all UK sailings including all ferries,

cargo vessels that carry passengers and cruise ships. Other features are holiday news items, *Funnel Vision* (an online maritime magazine), detailed information on shopping in Calais and points of interest around the port.

6
Sorting out the Formalities

CHECKING VISA AND PASSPORT REQUIREMENTS

Who needs a passport?

As a general rule, every traveller over 16 needs a passport; children under 16 can be included on a parent's passport. You are always asked to show your passport entering and leaving the UK. Transport providers such as airlines and ferry companies are responsible for checking that travellers have valid passports and will deny boarding to those who do not.

UK citizens travelling in Europe will find greatest variety in the standard of border control, particularly if driving. Many road border points are no longer manned, and some countries appear more concerned with selling motorway permits than checking passports. Some European countries ask for a valid motor insurance certificate to be shown by drivers entering the country as well as a passport.

UK Passport Agency

- IMPORTANT - Increase In Passport Fees
- British Visitor's Passport abolished
- Passports: General Advice
- Regional Passport Offices including latest turnround times
- New Passports
- Additions/Amendments to Passports
- Qualifications for UK Passport
- Passports: children/young people
- Getting Married
- Lost Passports
- Customers with disabilities
- Entry Visas
- Leaflets available

Fig. 26. The UK Passport Agency web site.

The UK Passport Agency has a web site (see Figure 26) which answers any questions you might have. Passports cannot be applied for on the web.

Check that:

☑ Your passport is up to date and will not expire whilst you are travelling; many countries require a passport that is valid for some months after your return.

☑ Children under 16 are on both parents' passports in case one is not able to travel.

☑ A photograph of your child is on the passport if required. Certain countries ask for this, including Algeria, Cameroon, Morocco, the Philippines, Saudi Arabia and some of the former Soviet Republics.

☑ Children over 16 have their own passport. If their 16th birthday occurs while they are travelling they will need their own passport for that trip.

☑ The names on the passport and tickets/insurance documents match.

☑ If you have a different surname from your husband/wife ask for a statement that explains this in your passport. This can be very useful if you are travelling to a country where there would be some unease at unmarried people sharing a room!

☑ Your passport does not contain the stamp of a country regarded as hostile by any country you intend to visit. If it does, it is normally possible to obtain a duplicate passport to smooth your path.

Who needs a visa?

Visa requirements change and depend on your nationality. It is your responsibility to have a valid visa. Visas can sometimes take a long time to process so apply as soon as you can. Most countries issue visas in advance but some make them available for purchase on arrival.

Information you read on passports and visas must be up to date. Sources of reliable information on and off the web include:

• embassies and High Commissions

• travel books and updates

• tourist information offices

• travel web sites

• travel agents.

LOOKING AT HEALTH ISSUES

Travel is so common that it is easy to forget about potential health risks. You can use the web to obtain up-to-date details of current health hazards and of preventative measures. There is always a chance that you might become ill or have an accident while abroad. Unless you are properly insured, it could turn out to be extremely expensive. You can use the web to check reciprocal arrangements and to compare the cost of holiday insurance. You can also get an overview of health issues for UK nationals from the Department of Health's web site.

Health advice for travellers

Contents

- Travel within Europe
- Form E111 - information
- Travel outside Europe
- Travelling for health treatment
- Basic health tips
- Latest Health Updates

Fig. 27. The Department of Health's web site.

Government health departments are a reliable source of information on health risks and give advice on necessary precautions and preparations. In the UK, the Department of Health produces a booklet *Health Advice for Travellers,* which gives detailed information on precautions, reciprocal agreements, and vaccinations. It contains Form E111 which entitles you to free or reduced cost emergency medical treatment in many EU countries. The booklet is free and can be obtained from main post offices or by phoning the Health Literature Line on 0800 555 777.

In addition to government advice many travel related sites have their own content on, or links to, health information for travellers. Travel Health Online, an American site with comprehensive, up-to-date content on health issues, is frequently linked to by travel web sites (see Figure 28).

By using *Travel Health Online*, you agree to comply with the Subscriber Agreement

General Travel Health Concerns

- Travel Health Overview
- Pre-Trip Planning
- Travelers with Special Concerns
- Preventive Vaccinations
- **Travel Precautions**
  - ☐ AIDS & Sexually Transmitted Diseases
  - ☐ Air Travel Concerns
  - ☐ Beach Safety
  - ☐ Cold and Heat Concerns
  - ☐ Food and Beverage Selection
  - ☐ Insect Protection
  - ☐ Motion Sickness
  - ☐ Safety Concerns
  - ☐ Sun Protection

Fig. 28. Travel Health Online: an excellent starting point
for research into possible perils.

CHECKING TRAVEL WARNINGS

Tourism now takes people to every corner of the globe. In some places
western tourists can encounter safety problems ranging from war and
terrorism to pickpockets. Government foreign office web sites are a
reliable source of information on current problems (see Figure 29). It
can be interesting to see how different governments interpret the same
situation. Advice is not just related to crime or warfare but can cover
extremes of weather or natural disasters.

General travel sites and travel books also deal with safety and
health. Many have special features on current concerns or topics such
as women travelling alone. Some are an excellent read – disaster
stories well told can make you feel a lot better about not going to
exotic places for your holidays. Newsgroups give you informal contact

with people who have been or live there. Potentially dangerous situations can develop or change quickly, and the Internet is a valuable aid to keeping up to date with developments from a range of sources. During the political disturbances in Indonesia in 1998, for example, updates for visitors were posted to several travel newsgroups and on web sites promoting tourism in the country.

To experience the really 'nasty places' from the safety of your computer visit Fielding's Dangerous Places (see Figure 30). They tackle it all with the blackest of humour. It's perceptive and practical, and probably the only travel book that persuades you to stay at home for your holidays.

Travel Advice Unit, Consular Division
  Foreign & Commonwealth Office

COLOMBIA

Violence and kidnapping remain serious problems in Colombia. In rural areas in particular there is a serious risk of being caught up in terrorist or guerilla attacks and opportunistic kidnapping. Four British citizens have been kidnapped since January 1995

Visitors should be extra vigilant travelling throughout Antioquia Department avoiding the Uruba region as well as the border area with Panama.

Visitors should always take advice from the British embassy, Bogota (tel: 317 6690) and local authorities before travelling by road, and should, if possible, avoid travel by vehicle away from major urban/tourist areas and routes, or outside daylight hours.

British Diplomatic Posts: contact details

Fig. 29. FCO ONLINE carries Travel Advice notices,
and some British consular information material.

Consular help

When serious problems occur while you are on holiday, your country's embassy has a duty to help. Consular help is however, limited. Details can be found on government web sites which give advice to travellers. The following applies specifically to British nationals but most embassies offer their citizens similar support.

Gimmeyawalletland
Imagine a naked man walking down the street with $100 bills taped to his body. That's what the typical tourist looks like to the residents of nasty places.

The fact that you consider yourself the owner of your camera, wallet, luggage, watch and jewellery is not really a debating point with many of these folks. The concept that you might need to be killed to expedite the transfer of those goods is a really minor detail to some. You don't need to be robbed in these places to lose your money, the police and officials will simply ask for it with a smile.

In many war-ravaged, impoverished countries, the only law is survival of the fittest or fastest. In some countries you will need criminals to protect you from the government.... In case you wonder where the most honest countries in the world are, they are Denmark, Finland, Sweden, New Zealand and Canada according to Transparency International. Here are a few tips to at least staunch the flow and escape with your body parts intact.

Fig 30. Fielding's Dangerous Places helps keep you safe.

Consuls can:
- ☑ Issue emergency passports.
- ☑ Contact relatives and friends to ask them to help you with money and tickets.
- ☑ Advise on how to transfer funds.
- ☑ In an emergency, advance money against a sterling cheque.
- ☑ As a last resort, and provided that certain strict criteria are met, make a repayable loan for repatriation to the UK.
- ☑ Help you get in touch with local lawyers, interpreters and doctors.
- ☑ Arrange for next of kin to be informed of an accident or death and advise on procedures.
- ☑ Contact and visit British nationals under arrest or in prison and, in certain circumstances, arrange for messages to be sent to relatives or friends.

☑ Give guidance on organisations experienced in tracing missing persons.

☑ Make representations on your behalf to the local authorities.

Fees are charged for some services.

Consuls cannot:

☒ Intervene in court proceedings.

☒ Get you out of prison.

☒ Give legal advice or instigate court proceedings on your behalf.

☒ Get you better treatment in hospital or prison than is provided for local nationals.

☒ Investigate a crime.

☒ Pay your hotel, legal, medical or any other bills.

☒ Pay for travel tickets for you except in very special circumstances.

☒ Undertake work more properly done by travel representatives, airlines, banks or motoring organisations.

☒ Obtain accommodation, work or a work permit for you.

☒ Formally assist dual nationals in the country of their second nationality.

CASE STUDIES

Chris applies for an E111

Chris is trying to keep the cost of his planned trip down. When he reads about the E111 on the Department of Health's web site he decides to apply for one and save on travel insurance for the European part of his trip. However, when he gets the details he realises that it alone would not cover him for all eventualities and on balance decides that he still needs health insurance cover, regardless of the cost. He decides to use the web to compare insurance policies and uses search engines to find insurance companies with web sites.

Tom investigates annual travel insurance

Involving all the family in researching travel options has certainly paid off in terms of holiday ideas. Tom's family has now got three trips abroad planned for the coming year. He decides to look at the option of multi trip insurance cover and uses the web and e-mail to get a range of quotes. The policy he chooses does not cost much more than he would have paid for cover for one trip. It also includes 17 days' skiing cover.

SITESEEING TIPS

Passports, visas and general information

Living Abroad Publishing
http://www.livingabroad.com
If you're about to go on a business trip or holiday to another country, this US publisher offers an e-mail question and answer facility on anything you need to know before you leave. Examples include: Do I need a visa if I plan to do business in France on a short-term basis? Is tipping a waiter necessary in Singapore? What are the business hours in Brazil?

Lonely Planet
http://www.lonelyplanet.com
Offer a 'survival kit to staying healthy (or at least upright) on the road' as well as links to sites covering insurance, visas and embassies.

The Embassy Page
http://www.embpage.org
Searchable site with links to most embassies and consulates in all parts of the world. Other useful links for travellers can be accessed from this site. FAQ and bulletin board.

UK Passport Agency
http://www.open.gov.uk/ukpass/ukpass.htm
Detailed and regularly updated information on passport application procedures, including current waiting times.

Health

Beach Cleanliness
http://www.environment-agency.gov.uk
The State of the Environment section provides objective, up-to-date statistics on bathing water quality for all British beaches. Maps show the location of beaches that meet, fail or exceed EU standards. For each beach there is frighteningly detailed information of what's in the water. If you want to avoid the largest faecal streptococci colonies on your holidays, pay a visit here first!

Department of Health (UK)
http://www.open.gov.uk/doh/hat/hatcvr.htm
Details of procedures and health related concerns for British nationals when travelling abroad.

Travel Health Online
http://www.tripprep.com/index.html
Health issues can be explored by country or specific illness on this web site. The summary of travel illness makes cautionary reading and the section on preventative medications and vaccines is reassuring. If you want to know what could get you and how to guard against it this is the place to go.

Travel warnings

Fielding's DangerFinder
http://www.fieldingtravel.com/df/index.htm
Even the disclaimer on this site makes good reading. It's entitled *A Polite Discourse on Liability (Ours) and Gullibility (Yours),* and reminds you that 'visiting these places may likely get you killed or earn you the nickname Stumpy. On the other hand, since more people are injured in their homes than outside them, you may be safer traveling.' It's more about how to avoid danger rather than find it, but if it's danger you're after there's no better guide. The site is primarily an advert for *The World's Most Dangerous Places* and other Fielding's travel books. It entices potential customers by making extracts and reviews available, a bit like letting you read the best bits of a book in the shop before you buy it. DangerFinder is well worth a visit, it's hard to believe anything so grim can be so funny. Books can be ordered online.

Foreign and Commonwealth Office (UK)
http://www.fco.gov.uk/travel
Has advice aimed at helping travellers avoid trouble or threats to their personal safety resulting from political unrest, lawlessness, violence, natural disasters, epidemics, anti-British demonstrations and aircraft safety. There is a list of countries that British travellers are advised not to visit, and a range of leaflets with practical tips for travellers to major tourist destinations. Users can create a 'personalised' home page and register for e-mail updates.

Other government sites include:
Consular Travel Advice (Australia)
http://www.dfat.gov.au/consular

CHILE

The Chilean government has recently passed a new law concerning cellular phone usage. The law states that people who are driving are prohibited from using their cellular phones while the car is in motion due to an increased number of automobiles accidents which have occurred reportedly while the driver was using a cellular phone. Forty-nine Chileans, known for their preoccupation with social status, were arrested for using cellular phone while driving. Police discovered later that at least a third of the cellular phones were artificial replicas. Although this event sounds unusual, visitors to the country should note that Chilean law forbids both citizens and foreigners from using a cellular phone while driving.

Fig. 31. Travel warnings can give interesting insights into your destination.

US State Department Travel Warnings & Consular Information Sheets
http://travel.state.gov/travel_warnings.html

Travelocity
http ://www.travelocity.com/kroll
This link to Kroll Associates' 'Top News for Top Travellers' has travel warnings, aimed at business travellers, that are updated daily. The information is varied and detailed – for example, details of planned strikes, political protests and adverse weather conditions.

Insurance
Top Insurance Sites in The UK
http://design.netvillage.co.uk/topsites/insurance/index.htm
Index providing links to a large number of insurance companies in the UK.

The Insurance Mall
http://www.theinsurancemall.co.uk
Searchable site which provides links to insurance and finance-related sites.

7
Doing Detailed Research on your Destination

Whatever you want to know about a place can probably be found on the Internet. Using a mixture of commercial concerns, official tourist information organisations, academic institutions and individuals who love travel and want to share their experiences, you'll be able to research destinations in depth. Whether it's Alton Towers or Antarctica, Butlins or Burkino Faso the Internet will give you an insight into what you can do and find in most places on earth.

USING OFFICIAL TOURIST INFORMATION

Tourism contributes to the economic well-being of many countries and most promote themselves through tourist information offices. Every part of the UK, for example, has a tourist board representing it. Official tourist information is usually quite detailed and comprehensive, but it is promotional, so rarely mentions anything negative about a place. Most tourist information offices have web sites (see Figure 32). The advantages of contacting them in this way are:

- ☑ Searchable web sites help you find just what you want.

- ☑ Many have an e-mail you can use for queries that aren't covered elsewhere.

- ☑ There are no postage or printing costs so it's cheaper for you and for the provider of the information.

- ☑ It removes the need to phone tourist information offices. Many can now only be reached by using premium rate phone numbers, sometimes in order to negotiate with a multi choice answer machine that never has quite the option you want.

- ☑ Many sites have connections to related information about an area or country. It's easy to follow links and get a more balanced and comprehensive picture of your chosen destination.

Fig. 32. A typical tourist board web site
(**http://www.cumbria-the-lake-district.co.uk**).

USING UNOFFICIAL TOURIST INFORMATION

Travellers themselves are the best providers of travel and tourist information. The Internet gives those wanting to share their experiences, good and bad, a global audience for virtually no cost. Aspiring travel writers no longer have to find a publisher, they can do it themselves and reach wider audiences than any book.

Some of the best material on the Internet comes from people who love travel. If they enjoyed somewhere they want others to have the same pleasure; if things went wrong they like to warn.

Sources of unofficial information
- newsgroups (see Chapter 9)
- mailing lists (see Chapter 9)
- bulletin boards or travelogues
- books
- newspapers.

Bulletin boards and travelogues
Many web sites related to travel have a bulletin/notice board or travel-

ogue section. These are often divided into sections that deal with particular interests or groups such as children, women travellers or those with special needs. Some discussion groups focus on particular destinations. Lonely Planet's site provides a good example of focused discussion groups, called The Thorn Tree (see Figure 4). It has various 'branches' covering all destinations and topics. The listings at the end of this chapter highlight other sites with similar facilities.

Books

Books remain an excellent source of information, and the Internet promotes and enhances their use by:

- Making updating easy and immediate. Many travel publishers make extensive use of their web sites for this.

- Enabling users to find and buy a huge range of books – particularly useful for more obscure ones. Internet bookshops are quick and easy to search and have huge stocks.

- Giving access to book reviews and the chance of writing reviews yourself.

- Making extracts and sometimes the whole book available on the web.

Newspapers

Reading the local paper for your holiday destination can give you a good feel for what the place is like. It lets you look at everyday information that can help you develop a better understanding, and plan your trip accordingly. Most national and many local papers have free web editions. Details of directories of newspapers available on the web are at the end of this chapter.

ACHIEVING THE RIGHT BALANCE

All the above provide a good counterbalance to official tourist information which has to treat all destinations in the country it represents as being of equal merit. Travellers in their personal accounts can 'tell it like it is'. This is particularly useful for anything slightly 'controversial' such as attacks, human or otherwise, on tourists that official information providers may play down. If, for example, you are concerned about bear attacks on walkers in North America or Canada, the official sources will provide you with good precautionary information, reassure you that attacks are rare and say that you are lucky to even see a bear. If you want to evaluate risks for yourself you can:

- use newsgroups and bulletin boards to ask the questions you want
- look at previous discussions on the topic
- find books on the issue
- find web sites that cover this topic
- find archived material in newspapers on actual events.

CHECKING THE WEATHER

Weather is the obsession of the British and one of the reasons people travel. The tradition for those living in cool countries is to go somewhere warm, whilst people who live in dry hot places often look for cool holiday destinations! Whatever your destination or intended activity you need an idea of what the weather is likely to be and the web makes that easy for you. There are many excellent weather related sites offering:

- current forecasts
- details of average conditions from archived data over several years
- live satellite images of world weather
- severe weather warnings
- health and safety precautions for extreme weather conditions.

The providers include National Met Offices, newspapers and TV channels, universities and interested individuals. Many travel and accommodation related sites incorporate links to local weather data in order to entice or reassure prospective visitors.

MAKING A PERSONALISED MAP

Providing online maps for free is a growing trend. Street maps and driving directions are mainly for addresses in North America, but new European sites are appearing all the time. A good one to keep an eye on is UK Street Map, which covers streets in London and provides detailed road maps, including camp site locations, for the rest of the country. A good map can show you a lot about your accommodation, for example, such as the proximity of busy roads or

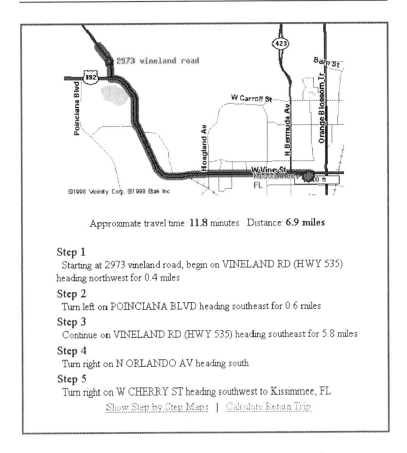

Approximate travel time: **11.8** minutes   Distance: **6.9 miles**

Step 1
Starting at 2973 vineland road, begin on VINELAND RD (HWY 535) heading northwest for 0.4 miles

Step 2
Turn left on POINCIANA BLVD heading southeast for 0.6 miles

Step 3
Continue on VINELAND RD (HWY 535) heading southeast for 5.8 miles

Step 4
Turn right on N ORLANDO AV heading south

Step 5
Turn right on W CHERRY ST heading southwest to Kissimmee, FL

Show Step by Step Maps | Calculate Return Trip

Fig. 33. Mapblast provides written directions or a detailed map
of any destination in the USA.

railways. Services like Mapblast (see Figure 33) include locations of commercial concerns such as take aways, service stations and shops.

The web is an excellent place to find and order traditional maps for most places in the world. State mapping services such as the UK Ordnance Survey have searchable sites with an online ordering facility, and there are several specialist map publishers and shops offering the same.

FINDING AND USING WEB CAMERAS

Webcams are cameras which transmit live or regularly updated images across the web. Many tourist destinations such as cable car top stations in the European Alps have shown live camera transmissions on local TV stations for years in order to encourage visitors. These are now being adapted for web transmission. The number available from around the world is staggering. You can watch the border crossing from Finland to Russia, keep an eye on the McDonalds queue in Stockholm, check live traffic details in most US cities, or get a good look at the snow conditions in many ski resorts. People have moved to live in cities they observed for a period of time through a web camera and liked the look of!

You can find web cameras sited:

- in theme parks and other tourist attractions
- at ski resorts
- on mountain tops
- in major tourist cities
- on surfing beaches
- at busy traffic intersections.

LEARNING THE LANGUAGE

What do you call someone who speaks two languages?
Bi-lingual.
What do you call someone who speaks only one language?
English!

Sadly this is still true of many English-speaking travellers abroad. If you do not know the language of the place you are visiting, you are much more likely to be swindled, misunderstood or ignored. You will get more out of your travels if you learn some language basics. Even a few phrases – please, thank you, go away and how much does this cost – can make a difference. Despite English being regarded by its speakers as the universal language, there are many more people who don't speak or understand it. If you try to speak the language of your host country, listeners are more likely to take pity on you, and in some cases reveal that they speak fluent English anyway!

Use the web to:

- find sites that offer free and priced language tuition

- download interactive dictionaries

- translate documents

- have a foreign phrase of the day e-mailed to you.

Newsgroups can be contacted to check how widely understood or acceptable a language is. Historical disagreements between nations can mean speakers of certain languages are less than welcome.

COMMERCIAL AND NON-COMMERCIAL TRAVEL SITES

Travel information on the web can be roughly divided into commercial and non-commercial provision, although many cross-link. Both have benefits for the traveller. Commercial sites can offer the chance to pick up a bargain and make all your arrangements with several clicks of the mouse. Many of the larger ones can be regarded as 'gateways' as they aim to offer links to everything they think travellers need. Non-commercial sites have a special value. On these nothing is being sold – experiences and information are being freely shared.

Commercial gateways
Typically these offer or link to a range of services including:

- online booking of transport, accommodation and entry tickets to attractions

- travel news and features

- competitions

- free electronic newsletters

- bulletin boards, discussion areas and live chat

- detailed destination information often including videos or live cameras

- maps

- weather information

- currency converters

- links to travel books and bookshops

- help with finding travel companions

- e-mail updates on bargain holidays and flights

- current flight arrival and departure information for major airports
- car rental.

The large gateways can be overwhelming and bombard you with flashing advertising banners which are slow to load on older computers and can cause them to crash. They do, however, give you a 'one stop shop'. If you don't mind having your content and links selected they can be a good place to start your research.

Which you go for is largely a matter of personal preference and what your software and hardware can cope with. Where online booking facilities are offered, SSL encryption is used (see Chapter 2) and therefore requires browser software that can cope with this such as Netscape 2, Explorer 3 or later.

Non-commercial gateways

These are generally compiled and maintained by individuals who love travel or are concerned by a particular aspect of it, *eg* Andreas Holmberg in Finland maintains Pistoff (**http://www.pistoff.com**) because he's interested in skiing, started this as a project at university and believes in the value of non-commercial web sites. Bill and Caroll Randall are keen to encourage disabled people to travel and have built a site (**http://www.access-able.com**) that promotes this (see Chapter 2). These sites are very personal and while they may have less content they often have more depth than commercial ones. The distinctions between the two groups are not always that solid, with links backwards and forwards, each helping users make the best of all that is available. Many non-commercial sites choose to keep their content simple (text only, frame free versions) which makes them accessible to people with older computers.

CASE STUDIES

Tom brushes up his French

Tom decides to set an example for the rest of the family by learning French before they go skiing. The children do it at school, but he knows they'll refuse to use it on holiday. He finds a site that will e-mail him a different phrase each day which is ideal as he doesn't have much spare time. He works out that he'll have time to learn 70 phrases before he goes.

Mary becomes a cyber traveller

Mary's first trip to Calais was a great success, she has now got a passport and an interest in foreign places. She knows that holidays abroad aren't really a possibility unless she can find a job that pays double what she's getting now. Even so, she likes hearing about other people's trips and decides to look at some of the travel discussion groups on the Internet. She learns about sites that offer virtual visits and is fascinated by those with live cameras, she almost feels she's there. Some of the holiday disaster stories she reads make her think that this is perhaps the best way to see exotic destinations.

Chris gets a 'postcard'

Chris gets a long e-mail from his parents in San Francisco. All their plans have gone smoothly so far, although his dad says the drive from Florida was longer than he remembered! His mum thanks him for the maps and driving directions he put together for them from the web, particularly the detailed ones of Florida, as she had been worried about getting lost and into trouble.

SITESEEING TIPS

Gateways

Cybertrip
http://www.cybertrip.com
Easy and quick to use. Geared for those starting from US, but with good worldwide links. Concentrates on links rather than its own content.

European Travel Network
http://www.etn.nl
ETN European Travel Network promotes worldwide travel and the use of discounted flights and hotels. It's crammed full of links, but normally quick to download. A place of serendipity, it feels slightly disorganised. Searching through it is rather like rooting through piles of bargains at a sale. It also has a section on travel jobs and one where homes for rent or exchange can be advertised for free.

Eurotrip
http://www.eurotrip.com
Magazine-format site with articles on budget travel in Europe. Includes European rail and bus information, details of budget accommodation, discussion boards, travel book reviews, advice for women travellers, a free newsletter and a cheap flight forum.

Excite Travel
http://www.city.net
Searchable database of over 5,000 destinations. Information is also organised by interest categories which include: Business Travel, Cruises & Tours, Family Travel, Food & Lodging, Sports & Outdoors.

Expedia
http://www.expedia.msn.com
Owned by Microsoft, Expedia aims to offer you a one-stop Internet shopping mall with a wide selection of travel goods and services. Travel wizards help you search for vacations by destination, origin and price, as well as for last-minute deals. At the moment many of the online booking services are only for Canada and the US but there are plans to extend this to Europe. Works best with latest browser software.

Leisure Planet
http://www.leisureplanet.com
The Lycos travel guide with flight, hotel and car hire booking facilities as well as comprehensive guide book information.

Rec.Travel Library
http://www.travel-library.com
Travel and tourism information with an emphasis on personal travelogues. Lots of practical information and links on where to go and how to get there. Most destinations are covered and there's information on bicycle travel as well as the more usual forms of transport. A good place to read about others' experiences and a chance to submit your own.

Travelling with Ed and Julie
http://www.twenj.com
Sites like this highlight the best of the Internet, people freely giving their time and experience. Ed and Julie Gehrlain invite you to 'browse away and take whatever might make your trip more enjoyable. In return, when you have the chance to help others enjoy your favourite spots, do it!' There are many interesting personal travelogues here, including a very detailed account of a vacation planned from the US to Europe using just the Internet.

Travelshop
http://www.travelshop.de
This searchable site is available in German and English (see Figure 34). It covers most destinations from the point of view of travellers starting from Europe. There are links to theme parks, as well as all airlines and railways in the world with web sites. There is a section on travel-related jobs offered and wanted.

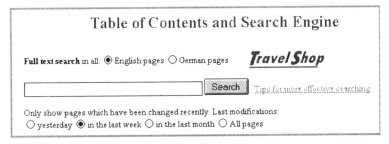

Fig. 34. Travelshop's efficient search engine helps you find what you want.

Tourismus Team Europe
http://www.tte.ch
Swiss site that offers a range of countries 'At your Fingertips' (see Figure 40). They specialise in Swiss and European destinations but have links worldwide. The site can be viewed in all the major European languages.

World Heritage List
http://www.unesco.org/whc/heritage.htm
The World Heritage Committee has a duty to publish and update a list of 'properties forming part of the cultural and natural heritage . . . that are recognised as exhibiting outstanding universal value'. In January 1998 the World Heritage List included 552 cultural and natural sites covering most countries in the world. Around 30 new sites are added each year. These 'properties' include provincial parks such as Dinosaur in Alberta, The Volcanoes of Kamchatka, The Old City of Berne in Switzerland, Hadrian's Wall, Durham Castle and Cathedral in the UK, Henderson Island in the Pitcairns, Auschwitz Concentration Camp in Poland, The Mill Network at Kinderdijk-Elshout in The Netherlands and Tongariro National Park in New Zealand. This site gives fast and functional access to compact factual information and provides links to paper and web-based reference material.

Official and unofficial tourist information
The first two sites listed will enable you to connect to most tourist information providers in the world, the rest are there to give a flavour of what you can find on the web.

ANTOR (Association of National Tourist Offices)
http://www.tourist-offices.org.uk
Provides links to sites offering tourist information for most places in the world, and details of UK-based carriers and tour operators who provide holidays to specific countries.

Tourism Offices World-wide Directory
http://www.towd.com
Guide to official tourist information from all over the world. The searchable index of nearly 2,000 entries lists only official government tourism offices, convention and visitors bureaux, and similar agencies. Search results show postal address, phone number and URL where available.

Antarctic Gateway
http://www.icair.iac.org.nz
This unusual destination seems to be growing in popularity. You can even access *The Antarctic Sun* newspaper at **http://asa.org/index.htm** If you can't afford an Antarctic journey, content yourself with a virtual tour of McMurdoe Sound at **http://astro.uchicago.edu/cara/ vtour** where you'll also find lots of background information.

Africa Dot Com
http://www.africa.com
Gateway to comprehensive information on Africa. Includes news, business, history, politics, education, sport, religion and health as well as travel and tourism. One of the links is to the Tanzania Tourist Board's chat room where you can discuss experiences and post questions. It is used to find pen pals, accommodation, shared transport, jobs and details of lion and tiger attacks!

Arab Net
http://www.arab.net
Dealing primarily with countries in the Middle East and North Africa, this searchable site covers all aspects of travel in that region (see Figure 35).

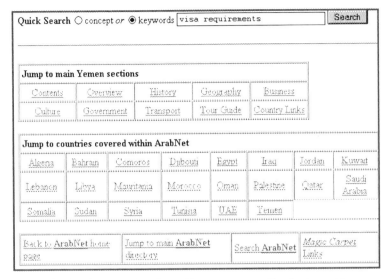

Fig. 35. A comprehensive online resource on the Arab world.

Bali Online
http://www.indo.com
Well organised site with destinations information and online reservation for all types of accommodation from the luxurious to the simple, often with discounts for online bookings.

The Best of Ireland
http://www.iol.ie/~discover/welcome3.htm
Wonderfully detailed guide to everything about Ireland. Available in French, German, Spanish and Italian. The usual travel and tourist information is supplemented with recipes, details of cybercafés, a business directory, information on politics and details of the lottery!

Dehli Gate
http://www.delhigate.com
Good source of information and links to Indian tourist information with an e-mail question and answer facility.

Events World-wide
http://www.eventsworldwide.com
From opera in Verona to world cup soccer, every major event is covered. Categories are Arts, Entertainment, Sports and Special,

which is everything else. Available in French, English, German, Italian and Spanish, it gives access to all the details you need, including booking information. Searchable by type of event, date or geographic location. Non-frames version available for users with older browsers. Smaller what's-on sites worth looking at include **http://www.whatsonstage.com** and **http://www.aloud.com** for music and theatre in the UK. They include reviews and online booking.

French Travel Gallery
http://www.bonjour.com
Detailed information on all things French with a very active on-site newsgroup.

Knowhere Guide
http://www.knowhere.co.uk
In their own words 'don't expect too many tourist post-card images here: Knowhere's a local's guide to the delights of a selection of towns in the UK and the Republic of Ireland, featuring the usual places to buy records, cheap food, comics and clothes, but also reports of buskers, street entertainers and skateboarders. So, be warned: this is NOT a standard tourist guide!' Most places in the UK described here, often in less than flattering terms.

Visit Britain
http://www.visitbritain.com
An example of the type of information most countries have on offer, this site is run by the British Tourist Authority. It covers most things visitors to Britain need to know including Britain for Walkers and Cyclists, which are searchable databases of suggested itineraries. There are lots of wonderful pictures that make it slow to load.

Maps

Mapblast
http://www.mapblast.com
Maps for USA and Canada with driving directions. You can mark on takeaways and other retail outlets. Links to local weather and news are also provided. Children and adults can have a lot of fun here.

MapQuest
http://www.mapquest.com
Offers users the ability to interactively zoom and browse their way to

over three million locations worldwide on an interactive atlas. Door-to-door driving directions are available for the US. The site came into being in February 1996, and now serves up over 1,000,000 maps per day. The Interactive Atlas offers international maps with views that can be magnified from national to street level.

Ordnance Survey
http://www.ordsvy.gov.uk
A much more serious and British approach to mapping. No gimmicks or free maps here yet, but you can view their products, use their links and muse over the difference between the USA and GB.

UK Street Map
http://www.streetmap.co.uk
Provides address searching and street map facilities for the UK. Currently street maps are for Greater London and there is an excellent road atlas map for the whole of mainland Britain.

Web cameras
Indexes for, and reviews of, a huge range of different cameras across the world can be found at:
http://www.cybertour.com
http://www.intelligent.com.au/webcam
http://www.windows2000.com

Hotel Bel Horizon, Val Thorens
http://www.belhorizon.com
A particularly nice camera that shows conditions on the pistes rather than just a summit view. The hotel owner Antoine Desvallees says he started doing it so his children couldn't say, 'Hey Dad, you do not even know what the Internet is!' Users can vote by e-mail which way the camera should be pointed the next day! There are excellent links to a range of other web cameras and indexes, as well as detailed weather and snow reports and resort information. The site is in English and French and offers a facility for hotel guests to keep in touch with each other and the owners. If you want to convince yourself that you need a ski holiday have a look at this one!

Nettours
http ://www.nettours.co.at
Twenty-eight live web cameras for Austria.

Topin
http://www.topin.ch
Live European tourist and weather cameras. A mixture of Swiss
mountain resorts and European cities with links to additional tourist
information. They have a project called Topgolf planned which will
do something similar for golf courses.

The Waikiki Aquarium Coral Cam
http://waquarium.mic.hawaii.edu
Live cameras of visitor attractions are becoming more common, you
can watch the fish (the image changes every ten seconds), and read
factual information on what you see. Another good site for live
cameras is Disney **(http://www.disney.com).**

Checking the weather
Live cameras are a good way of seeing what it's like now but if you
want forecasts or historical data try:

Scottish Avalanche Information Service
http://www.sais.gov.uk
Excellent site. Links to other weather and avalanche sites. Daily
forecasts of climbing conditions in Scotland (see Figure 9).

UK Meteorological Office
http://www.meto.gov.uk
Current and historical weather details, information on how weather
forecasts work and how to work in weather forecasting, links to all
other national meteorological services and quality weather sites in the
world make this a fascinating place to visit.

US National Weather centre
http://www.nws.fsu.edu
An excellent starting point for exploration of weather sites on the web
which have significant current or past weather information. Satellite
images, weather maps and movies, climate information, earthquake
and hurricane reports, make this an incredible resource. There is a
text-only version.

Learning the language

Alta Vista
http://babelfish.altavista.digital.com
Not really a language-learning resource but it can sometimes help (see

Figure 44). The free translation facility is provided by Systranet (**http://www.systranet.com**) who offer more extensive, but priced services on their site.

Foreign Languages for Travellers
http://www.travlang.com
An interactive phrase book with sounds! Select the language you speak, and the language you want to learn (see Figure 36). That enables you to choose categories of words and phrases that are useful to travellers. Sound files are labelled with their size and you can choose whether to download them or not. Quizzes, pronunciation guides, links to related destination information and interactive dictionaries are additional features, and it's all for free. Users are encouraged to help expand the site and contribute to sound files.

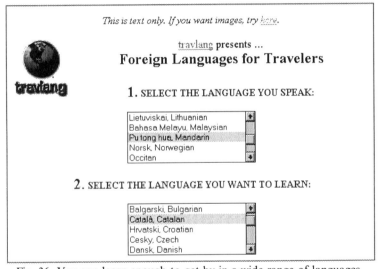

Fig. 36. You can learn enough to get by in a wide range of languages.

University of California at Berkeley
http://www.itp.berkeley.edu/~thorne/humanresources.html
Excellent resource which aims to 'lend starting points for mining the WWW for foreign language/culture specific resources ... a quality-only index ... we have sought to include only the best of the foreign language ('foreign' for native speakers of English) web sites out of the many that exist'. Invaluable for travellers as well as those with an academic interest in languages.

Newspaper directories

E&P Directory of Online Newspapers
http://www.mediainfo.com/emedia
Claims to be the most comprehensive reference resource of its kind. It includes newspapers that are on the web as well as those available through proprietary online services. Web-based papers are listed by country, for the US they are also listed by state. You can search for a specific publications, locations or attributes.

World Newspapers
http://www.dds.nl/~kidon/papers.html
This Dutch site has listings of and links to all the world's major newspapers.

8
Getting Connected – a Beginner's Guide

WHAT YOU NEED

To connect and make full use of the Internet you need:

- a computer
- a modem
- a telephone
- software for using the world wide web, e-mail, newsgroups and chat.

If you don't have your own equipment there are lots of possibilities for using someone else's. Although communicating via the Internet and obtaining information from it is often cheaper than using other sources and facilities, it can be very expensive to get started if you don't already own a computer.

PUBLIC INTERNET ACCESS POINTS

If you just want to use the Internet occasionally there are a growing number of places that offer public access to the Internet. In some cases access can be free, particularly when it is part of a training course. Otherwise you pay for time spent online. This represents good value for the occasional user as it removes the need to invest in costly hardware. Places where you can get access to the Internet include:

Libraries
Many offer Internet access and short courses to get you started. They normally charge around £5 an hour.

Schools
Both primary and secondary schools are opening up their computer facilities, which increasingly include Internet access, to the public. This is normally outside school hours and can be linked to training

and child care. Check with your Local Education Authority for details of such schemes in your area.

Universities
Many make facilities available to the public in conjunction with short courses to help you get started.

Cybercafés
These are places where you can eat, drink and access the Internet. You'll find them in *Yellow Pages*, usually listed under computer services. Prices for online time tend to be higher than libraries. Internet Magazine offers a listing of Cybercafés in the UK on their web site.

Schemes promoting computer literacy
There are a number of local and national schemes. In the UK an initiative called IT FOR ALL offers a free, easy-to-read guide on all aspects of information technology and details of courses and computer access points in your locality. Contact them on 0800 456 567.

Programmes related to IT
Look out for these in the media. The BBC, for example, runs an annual campaign in the UK called Computers Don't Bite. This is a month of co-ordinated events and programmes. It includes taster sessions all over the country in libraries, colleges, careers centres, shopping centres, buses and pubs. The free magazine produced to publicise it is an excellent introduction to all aspects of computing.

Friends and relatives
People with Internet access are often happy to share their discoveries with you, particularly if you cover the costs of online time and offer to find a holiday for them in return for using their computer!

Advantages of public access

☑ You don't have to invest in a computer, pay for a subscription with a service provider or sort out technical problems.

☑ Places that offer public Internet access are likely to have someone there who can help you if you get stuck.

☑ Public providers often have cheap or free courses on Internet use.

☑ If you're paying according to the time you spend online it stops you getting distracted and pushes you into using the time in a focused and productive way.

Disadvantages of public access

☒ It's not always available at the times you want. You may need to book in advance.

☒ It's not very private. Computers are always sited in visible locations so that their use can be supervised to some extent. Web pages are very colourful and tend to draw the eye of anybody passing.

☒ You will probably not be able to bookmark your own sites.

☒ You may not be able to browse for free offline. It's worth raising this with whoever is providing access, to see if you can arrange to do so for free, or for a reduced cost.

☒ There may be problems over receiving personal e-mail. This can be overcome by using a free web-based e-mail address.

USING YOUR OWN COMPUTER

If you have bought a computer recently it will probably have every-thing you need for connection to the Internet, a modem and browser software, as part of its standard package. If you don't have a modem you can buy one for around £100 and browser software is often free. If you are using an older computer, check that its speed and memory will be able to cope with the demands you'll be putting on it. You need at least 8MB of RAM and 12MB free hard disc space. Most computers bought over the last few years will have this and it's possible to upgrade computers relatively cheaply. The service provider you use to set up your connection to the Internet will be able to advise you if your computer is suitable.

Choosing a modem

A modem is the piece of hardware which allows your computer to communicate via the phone system. If you need to buy a modem, the main thing to look for is its speed. The faster your modem and computer are, the quicker you will receive and send data. This minimises time spent online which usually has a cost attached to it. The most reliable sources of up-to-date information on equipment are articles and adverts in the many Internet magazines (see Figure 37). These are available in paper form or on the web.

Modems

Top 10 Modems
Access comparative charts and reviews from the latest
issue of *PC World.*
Reviews Internal, External
Charts Internal, External

Complete Guide to Modems
Make an informed buying decision and examine our
exclusive list of product reviews and comparison
charts covering every modem we've tested since
September.

* External Modems
* Internal Modems

Modem Reviews, News and Tips
Read the latest single-product and comparative
reviews, news and tips.

Fig. 37. Computing and Internet related magazines offer
help with choosing the right hardware.

A modem can also act as an answering and fax machine when
linked to your computer. This is independent of the Internet and a
valuable extra resource, so check for these facilities.

CHOOSING AN INTERNET SERVICE PROVIDER

Once you have your modem and computer you need an Internet
Service Provider (ISP). This is usually a commercial organisation
which allows you to access its powerful computers from your smaller
one. When you connect to the Internet your first call is to your ISP,
and should only be at local call rates. They connect you to the rest of
the world. You normally pay a fee to your ISP for this service,
however, the free Internet access service announced by the Dixons

group may change all this. Fees, services offered, efficiency and customer support vary. Internet magazines usually have detailed up-to-date lists of who provides what and for how much. They also publish surveys on their relative performance. Providers fall into two main categories those which provide an online service and those which just provide access to the Internet.

Service providers

Companies like AOL, CompuServe, Microsoft Network and Line One provide a range of extra services which are exclusive to their members. This can include news, travel and weather information. These services offer an easy introduction to the web as they select and categorise sites for you, but are often more expensive than general providers like Demon, Virgin and Pipex. Avoid taking out a long term subscription before you've tried the provider out first. Most offer free trials so you can see how they compare with each other.

Questions to ask

When selecting a provider you should check the following:

Do they have a local Point of Presence (POP)?
Most do, and this means that your connection to the Internet is always at local call rates.

Do they offer a free trial?
It's the best way of finding out if they suit your needs. A free trial is only free in terms of the cost of using their computers, you still have to pay for the phone calls. 'Unlimited free access' means access to their computers. Once you are paying a subscription, that only covers the cost of using their computers too. Any time spent online (connected to the phone) appears on your phone bill.

Does the speed of their modems match the speed of yours?
If not transfers could be slow.

What ratio of modems to users do they have?
If it is high, *eg* 1:20, they may be engaged when you try to get through. A ratio of 1:10 is fairly standard. The lower it is, the better.

How easy are they to contact?
Despite what some of the publicity says, installation is not always straightforward and problems do occur once you're connected too.

You will probably need to ring their helpline at some point. Some providers offer 24-hour helplines; others have limited contact hours.

How are the help and customer service lines accessed?
Some ISPs have free numbers for initial contact, but national or even premium call rate numbers for contact once you have signed up. Several combine this with the expensive practice of answering the phone promptly, offering you a long list of pre-recorded choices, then playing soothing music interspersed with frequent apologies for keeping you waiting. To be avoided!

Can you can e-mail them with queries?
This can be very useful (unless your query is about why your e-mail's not working). It gives you time to think and try out suggestions.

What is the minimum subscription period?
Some of the prices quoted are based on committing yourself to a whole year's subscription. You should not do this without trying them out first. If you do choose this option check how long they've been in the business, how many users they have and what happens to your annual subscription if they go out of business.

Do they offer reduced rates for limited time per month access?
Most have this option which is useful if you are a light user. Paying for extra time can be expensive.

Do they offer free browser and other software?
Some charge an initial connection/set-up fee to include the browser and other software. It's worth checking if they include news reading, e-mail and chat software. Most do.

How many newsgroups do they give you access to?
Most providers give access to all the Usenet groups, well in excess of 26,000!

Do they offer free web space?
You may wish to create your own web page – it's surprisingly easy!

UNDERSTANDING AND EVALUATING THE COSTS

There are two main areas of cost to consider when you are using the Internet:

1. The subscription you pay to your service provider
2. Your phone bill: time you spend online incurs phone charges if you pay for local calls.

Provider A

Subscription type	Connection charge	Subscription	Equivalent monthly cost (all prices exclude VAT)
	£	£	£
Annual	FREE	107.88	8.99
Quarterly	FREE	32.50	10.83
Monthly	9.99	11.99	11.99

Provider B

£5.95 per month (£6.99 inc.VAT) – 10 hours online each month
£10.00 per month (£11.75 inc. VAT) – 100% unlimited access
1 month discount for annual payment
No set-up fees

Provider C

Two years' Internet use – no newsgroups	£30
Two years' Internet use and newsgroups	£40
Five years' Internet use and newsgroups	£75
e-mail @ 99p a week	

Fig. 38. Comparing service provider charges.

ISP charges

Some providers offer cheap basic services which suit casual users. Remember to check if the price quoted includes VAT. The main options on offer are:

Unlimited access packages
These allow you to connect to the Internet through your ISP for as long as you like. You pay the phone company for the time you spend online.

Limited access/low user packages
These give you a set amount of time each month with charges for extra time.

Electronic mail only
For those that require access to the Internet for electronic mail only.

Accounts typically include up to five electronic mail boxes and cost around £5 a month.

THE WORLD WIDE WEB

The web is the glossy multimedia magazine component of the Internet with information from all over the world on every subject, presented in an attractive way. The information is linked in a way that gives it a web-like structure; by following connections you go to related information. You can look at things in greater depth and make connections you might not otherwise have thought of, but it can also mean that you end up going round in circles, feeling trapped and frustrated. In theory you can find everything you would ever want, with the click of a mouse. In practice you need to spend a little time developing efficient search techniques in order to utilise the tremendous potential it offers.

Web sites and web pages
The world wide web contains millions of web sites. A web site is a collection of documents known as web pages that have been put together by a person or organisation. Each page has links that take you to related information. This could be to another page on the same site or to another site in a different part of the world. Links can be shown as coloured, underlined text or a picture. Clicking on a link takes you to the new site or page.

Skills needed
You don't need to know much about computers to use the web. Basic keyboarding skills are enough, the screens you work with are similar to those on word processors. What you do need to learn is how to search effectively for the information you want and avoid being swamped by irrelevant material.

UNDERSTANDING YOUR BROWSER

Browser software
When you use the web, you explore it using a browser. This is point and click software that helps you move around the web. You can browse through interconnected documents that can have their origin in any part of the world. Many new computers have browsers included as part of their start up software. When you sign up with an ISP they will provide you with the software you need. Some do this for

no charge, others charge a one off set-up fee. Once you have an Internet connection you can download the browser software of your choice from the web.

Netscape's Free Downloads and Software Upgrades

Welcome to Netscape's automatic software upgrade page! In three easy steps you'll be able to confirm your existing Internet software configuration, review our recommendation for upgrading to the very latest Netscape Internet software, and begin downloading the recommended upgrade - for FREE!

 Netscape Navigator and Communicator Standard Edition are now free! Or purchase Communicator Professional Edition for just $29.

 Do You Need to Upgrade? Download the latest version of Communicator for FREE!
You appear to be running:

- **Netscape Navigator 2.02E-VN006: Windows 3.1: English**

A later version of this software has been released. To take advantage of the latest Web software, you should upgrade to:

- **Netscape Communicator 4.05: Windows 3.1: English (40-bit encryption)**
  (File size is 12 MB; estimated download time on a 28.8 Kbps modem is 78 minutes)

If you are interested in downloading **different software or preview release software**, see the Overview of Products for download links to all Netscape software.

Fig. 39. You can compare the basic versions of browsers
to see which you prefer.

Navigator or Explorer

The web pages shown in this book are viewed using both Netscape Navigator and Microsoft Internet Explorer. Figures 3 and 40 show two versions of Netscape Navigator, Figure 44 shows Internet Explorer 3. They have slightly different icons and commands, but perform the same functions and are similar in appearance.

Like everything else associated with the Internet, browsers are continually being upgraded. If you want to keep up to date with developments look at **http://www.browsers.com** which is devoted to just that. It is not necessary to have the most up-to-date browser. In some cases an older computer may not be powerful enough to run the latest software.

Understanding web pages

The layout of a web page is similar to that of most word processed documents (see Figure 40).

- The security icon shows you the status of the document you are viewing. This document is insecure as the padlock is open. On some browsers the security icon is a key (see Figure 3).

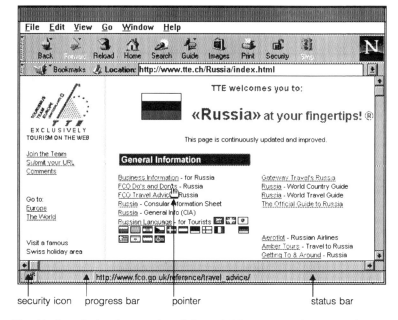

security icon   progress bar   pointer   status bar

Fig. 40. A typical web page viewed through Netscape Navigator Version 4.

- The progress bar fills with colour as a transmission is being made.

- The pointer moves round the page – use it to click on words, images, or the scroll bar.

- The pointer changes from an arrow to a finger when it is placed over a link.

- Links are usually coloured, underlined text or a picture.

- The status bar lets you know where clicking on a link will take you to and what the speed of current transmission or file size is.

Using the commands

You can look at browser software such as Netscape Navigator and Internet Explorer without being online. Spending time offline getting used to the layout and functions of your browser costs nothing. In addition there are certain things like sorting out bookmarks or composing e-mail that you can do offline. Then when you do go on-line, you will be familiar with the common commands and able to work quickly.

The commands which allow you to change settings and move around the web are at the top of the screen.

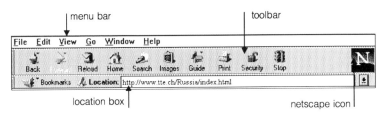

Fig. 41. Browser commands and menus.

Commands in the **menu bar** enable you to carry out a range of functions including:

● changing the appearance of your screen

● preventing the automatic loading of images

● printing

● copying and pasting text

● searching for a specific word in the displayed document.

You can look at how to use and alter these settings without needing to connect to the Internet.

The **toolbar** provides quick links to most popular commands from the menu bar. The commands are activated by a single click of the mouse. When their use is not available to you the icons are greyed out. Figure 41 shows the toolbar in picture and text form. It can also be displayed as just pictures or just text. On the newer browsers, allowing your pointer to dwell on a toolbar button will display its function.

The **back** button takes you to the previous page you were viewing.

The **forward** button takes you to the next open page and can only be used after going back.

The **reload** button reloads your current page: this is useful if a transfer of information has been interrupted or corrupted or you want to update it.

The **home** button takes you to your home page. This is the first page you connect to when you access the web. It is normally set by the ISP to take you to their site, but you can change it to a page of your choice either on the web or from your existing computer files. You could, for example, set it to always open your bookmark file rather than trying to connect to a web site.

The **search** button takes you to search engines.

The **images** button is only displayed if you have selected the option not to load images automatically. Clicking it will load the images for the current page.

The **guide** button activates a pop up menu of links to tools for finding Internet information.

The **print** button prints the current web page. A web page can be any number of screen or paper pages long. The print dialogue box, which appears after you have clicked on this icon, allows you choose whether to print specific pages or the whole document.

The **security** button allows you to check security information such as encryption status.

The **stop** button is useful when transfers are taking too long and you wish to terminate that particular connection. Keep an eye on the status bar at the bottom of the screen to see the progress of transmissions. Your modem has the potential to operate at up to 56 kbps, but information is sometimes received at less than 1kbps.

The **bookmarks** link enables you to go directly to sites you've previously added.

The **location box** gives you the 'address' or URL of the web page you are viewing.

The **Netscape icon** becomes animated when data is being transmitted.

Help pages
All the software has help sections. Print help pages that deal with topics relevant to your needs and use them to explore the facilities your browser offers without connecting to the Internet. If you're using a public access point, explain what you are doing and ask for free time to do it. As you are accessing the computer's hard disc rather than going online, it should not incur the same charge.

COPING WITH URLS

The World Wide Web is made up of a huge number of sites. Each site and each page has its own unique address known as a Uniform Resource Locator (URL). In order to visit a site you need to know its URL and enter it in the location box. There are various ways in which you can do this:

• You can type the URL directly into the location box and press enter.

• If you arrive at a page or site via a hypertext link you may not know its URL, but will see it displayed in the location box. Develop a habit of bookmarking any that are useful, so that you can access them again easily.

• If you are using Netscape you can enter URLs into your bookmark file offline. When you select a bookmark, the URL will automatically be transferred to the location box.

Efficiently organised bookmarks make an enormous difference to effective use of the web. Time spent doing this is easily repaid later. Details relating to organisation of bookmarks will be in the browser's help pages.

The importance of accuracy

URLs are like phone numbers, they only work if you get them exactly right. It is worth taking time to understand what they are made up of and what might be going wrong if you can't connect with the site you want. Getting error messages saying the URL you've just typed in doesn't exist is frustrating and time wasting. The accuracy needed extends to whether you use upper or lower case letters, where you put your full stops and what sort of slash or dash you use. At its simplest a URL looks something like this: **http://www.vauxhall.co.uk**

What it all means
http Stands for **Hypertext Transfer Protocol**. It is always followed by :// and tells your browser what type of document you want. For normal web documents you do not need to enter it as part of the address, the browser assumes that if you enter nothing, http:// should be there. Other commonly used protocols are ftp:// and news://. Secure sites start with https://.

www.vauxhall. This is known as the **domain name** and tells you the name of the server and company/organisation/individual you are connecting to.

co. Tells you what sort of organisation it is. Commonly used ones are:

co.   = commercial company in the UK
com. = commercial company elsewhere in the world and increasingly in the UK
ac.   = academic institution in the UK only. Elsewhere it is denoted by edu
gov. = governmental organisation
org. = other types of organisation
mil. = military site
net. = internet service provider

uk This tells you in which country the site originates. Every country has its own code, *eg* fr = France; is = Iceland; ie = Ireland; za = South Africa; pl = Poland. USA web sites do not normally use a country code. Resist the temptation to put a full stop at the end of a URL, there never is one!

The basic URL will generally take you to the **home page** of a web site. These provide content lists or site maps to help you find your way around the site.

Finding specific files

URLs that extend beyond the country code are the addresses of specific pages or files. They are usually separated from the main body of the URL by a / (forward slash) *eg* **http://www.vauxhall.co.uk/ skinet/skititle.htm** is a series of pages with the latest ski reports and snow conditions.

Specific files like these can change. If a URL is taking you to a current piece of information that file may disappear when information is updated and trying to reach it will result in an error message. If this happens, try going back to the address in the location box and deleting back as far as first forward slash.

Mistakes are often made when URLs are typed, sites move and disappear. It can be frustrating when you've read about a site that answers your questions and then you can't find it. At best there will be a message in the form of a hypertext link that will take you to the new address. If not you should be able to find a site's new location by searching for the site name or the topic it deals with using a **search engine** or **web directory.**

SELECTING SEARCH TOOLS

Unlike other libraries of information there is no single classification system on the WWW. It would be impossible to make use of this huge body of information without some index. Search engines, directories and meta crawlers act as index and contents pages for web information. They are powerful tools that can help you find what you want. Many have enthusiastic sounding names like Yahoo, Yell and Excite; they do behave in an enthusiastic manner, quickly fetching lots of interesting things for you to look at. This can cause problems. You can get hundreds, thousands, even millions of documents if your search is too general and none if it's too specific. Searches only take a few seconds to perform, even if they return a huge number of matches.

Search engines, directories and metacrawlers

- **Search engines**, which are also called 'spiders' or 'crawlers,' run automatically and visit web sites on the Internet in order to catalogue them. This means that they are constantly updating their content. They search on word match rather than contextual information and this results in a lot of irrelevant documents. Advanced searching techniques can help overcome this.

- **Directories** are compiled by humans. Sites are submitted by their authors and assigned to an appropriate category. This means they often produce better results than search engines in terms of relevance, but are sometimes less up to date.

- If you are having difficulty finding information on a subject you could try a **metacrawler**. These are programs that allow your query to be sent to several search engines and directories at once.

Most ISPs provide a link to one of the large search engines through a directory button. Alternatively you can use one of your choice by typing in the URL of the engine or directory you want in the location box.

Searching successfully

The directory Yahoo is a good place to start (see Figure 42). It has an excellent travel section and offers links to other engines and direct-

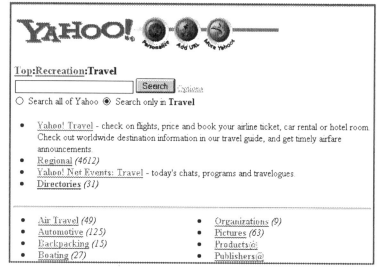

Fig. 42. Directories such as Yahoo let you limit your
search to a specific subject category.

ories, so if your Yahoo search is not successful, you can forward your
query to another search tool.

Travel-related sites abound on the web. You are likely to be
swamped rather than experience a shortage of places to visit.

- Try the same query with a few search tools to see how they compare
  (see Dogpile at the end of this chapter).

- Look at what they find and how they present it.

- Read the help section on refining or expanding searches,
  experiment with the techniques suggested.

Most search engines offer users the choice between concentrating on a
particular country or searching worldwide. Yahoo, for example, has
specific search engines for the UK, Germany, France, Italy, Norway,
Sweden, Japan, Korea, Asia, Canada, Australia, New Zealand and
all the states of the US. You access them by clicking on 'More
Yahoos'.

In addition to engines which search the whole of the web, large sites
with thousands of pages often have their own (see Figure 43).

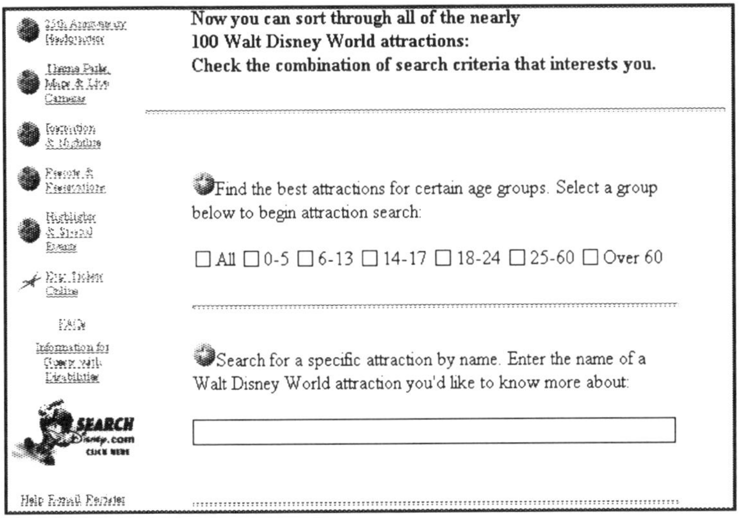

Fig. 43. Large sites such as Disney World have their own search engines.

SITESEEING TIPS

Netscape Navigator
http://www.netscape.com
Internet Explorer
http://www.microsoft.com/ie
Downloads, upgrades, anything you might ever want to do with a
browser can be done on these sites. Projected download times are
usually given.

Alta Vista
http://altavista.digital.com
Search engine with lots of interesting features, including a facility to
translate documents or your own text. It will translate phrases or
whole web pages from English to French, German, Spanish, Italian
or Portuguese and vice versa at amazing speeds. It is not always
idiomatic but nevertheless needs to be seen to be believed (see Figure
44). The translation facility can be accessed directly at:
http://babelfish.altavista.digital.com

Excite Search
http://www.excite.com
One of the biggest search engines. Also offers free e-mail.

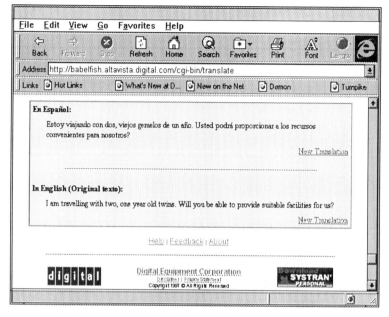

Fig. 44. Babel Fish offers a speedy translation service.

HotBot
http://www.hotbot.com
Powerful search engine of similar size to Excite. Claims to update daily and search results show the date written.

Dogpile
http://www.dogpile.com
A multi-engine search tool which 'fetches' links for you to look at. Searches web sites and newsgroups. You can even arrange the order in which the 20 + engines and directories it searches are visited. Use it to look at how different engines respond to the same search.

If you want to know more about searching the web or access tutorials on it, look at **http://www.searchenginewatch.com** for a thorough examination of the subject and links to similar sites. You can register for a free e-mail newsletter to keep you up to date with search tool developments.

NetMind Services
http://www.netmind.com/index.html
A free service which allows you to register the URLs of web pages that are important to you. It visits your registered pages regularly and reports back to you by e-mail whenever one of them changes. You can also register searches with some search engines. It performs the searches for you and sends you an e-mail when the result of the search changes.

Internet magazine
http://internet-magazine.com
One of the many publications that deal with this subject. This magazine's web site lists, evaluates and links to all the major UK ISPs and gives details of their charges. Clicking on Info Please will bring up a mail composition window enabling you to enquire about an ISP's service by e-mail. It also has a list of all UK cybercafés.

internet *magazine*	Back to IAP Central	**Key**			
	Back to Home Page	**LLO** - leased line only			
		ISDN/LLO - ISDN & leased line only			
ISPs - submit your details here!		*- inc VAT			
		** - annual price inc VAT			
FULL UK COVERAGE	**Tel No**	**Email**	**Cost**	**Backbone**	
Cyberscape	(01253) 724 000	Info Please	£12	Cable Internet / ISPC	
Datanet	(01252) 810 081	Info Please	£12.50	Planet Online	
Demon Internet	(0181) 371 1234	Info Please	£10	Demon	
DIALnet	(0800) 881 881	Info Please	£9	Cable Internet	
Direct Connection	(0181) 297 2200	Info Please	£11.49	BTnet / UUNET	
Direct Net @ccess	(01232) 330 311	Info Please	£7.50	GX Networks	
Easynet	(0171) 681 4444	Info Please	£9.90	Easynet / BTnet	
EDI	(01539) 731 000	Info Please	£15	Planet Online	
Entanet	(0500) 368 263	Info Please	£9	VBCnet	

Fig. 45. Internet magazine's list of all UK Internet service providers.

Yahoo
http://www.yahoo.com
http://www.yahoo.co.uk (for just British sites)
Search directory with well organised sections on a wide range of topics. Gives access to text-based information, chat sessions, and message boards.

Yahooligans
http://www.yahooligans.com
Part of Yahoo, geared towards children's needs and interests.

Freeserve
http://www.freeserve.net
This could be the start of an entirely new approach to encouraging increased use of the Internet. Part of the Dixons retail group, Freeserve offers unlimited Internet access, e-mail and newsgroup facilities without charge. All you pay for is your online time. Calls to the technical support unit, however, cost £1 a minute, so if you need telephone help it could end up costing you more than access through one of the other providers. Online technical support is available once you're connected. Freeserve is only available in the UK and the software is for Windows 95 or 98. Installation discs can be obtained from any store in the Dixons group.

9
Using the Internet Effectively and Economically

GETTING THE MOST FROM E-MAIL

If the only thing you ever used the Internet for was e-mail, it would justify establishing a connection in itself. Not only is it a cheap and efficient way of communicating with others, but it gives you access to masses of free information invaluable to travellers through mailing lists, e-zines (electronic magazines) and electronic newsletters. It is not surprising that it's the most widely used tool on the Internet.

The software for it comes as part of your connection with an ISP, and it is possible to have an e-mail only connection. Everyone with an Internet account can have a personal e-mail address, and there are free e-mail accounts available.

How it works

Messages are stored on the ISP's computer in a personal post box and can be collected at any time. As the initial connection is to a local number it's a very cheap and effective way to send things. In most cases, messages can be composed offline, stored and sent together during cheap rate for phone calls. How long they take to transmit depends on their length, but five short messages to five different countries can easily be sent in under a minute.

Advantages

- ☑ You can send messages, and attach pictures, documents and even sounds to anyone else who has an e-mail address.
- ☑ It is easy to send copies of the same message to different people.
- ☑ There is no need to worry about time zones, an e-mail sent in the middle of the night doesn't wake anyone.
- ☑ Material arrives in pristine condition.
- ☑ Messages and attachments can be printed off or stored on a computer.
- ☑ It costs the same to send whatever the destination.

☑ Where an e-mail can't be delivered it is generally returned to the sender with an explanation of the problem.

☑ Language difficulties that are exaggerated by the phone are minimised by e-mail.

Disadvantages

☒ You have to pay to look at your e-mail because you go online to receive it.

☒ E-mail is not always totally reliable. Mail can disappear completely, pretty much like conventional mail, although this happens only rarely.

☒ Messages are usually transferred quickly but graphics can take a long time. You can instruct your browser not to accept e-mails above a certain size.

Subject lines

What your recipient initially sees on their screen is your name and the subject matter of your message. It is important to fill in the subject line so that there is some indication of what you are writing about. If that person gets a lot of unsolicited mail, then they are likely to ignore messages with no subject line.

USING FREE SERVICES

E-mail

If you don't have an Internet account, or frequently change providers, there are several companies who offer free e-mail accounts. The pages you access to use e-mail have adverts for a range of services and the company gets its revenue from them. These adverts can be distracting, but are worth putting up with for the benefit of getting a free e-mail address that won't change when you change provider.

It is normally possible to access your free e-mail account from any computer with an Internet connection, using a name and password unique to you. This is useful for keeping in touch with people when you're travelling. The main disadvantage is that, because it is web-based, you have to be online to read and compose messages. You can get round this to a certain extent by composing your message in a word processing package, copying it to the clipboard, then pasting it in whilst online.

Forwarding services

Some providers of free e-mail addresses act as forwarders as well. This means that they automatically send on mail from your free address to any e-mail address you nominate. The result is that you can have one e-mail address that will not change regardless of how many times you change provider. You can use it in conjunction with your browser's e-mail software and therefore carry out most functions offline.

UNDERSTANDING E-MAIL ADDRESSES

Typical addresses will look like this:

> nomad@free-mail.com
> irene@serviceprovider. net
> ik@hols4u.co.uk

They are similar to URLs and require the same attention to accuracy. The first part of the address is the name you choose for yourself. It may not always be your first name or initials because once a name has been allocated it cannot be used by anyone else. If the name you want has been taken, you have to use a certain amount of imagination and ingenuity in choosing one to represent you. Some providers allocate numbers rather than names. Your name or number is always followed by @ (at). The next part shows who your account is with and follows the same conventions as URLs (see Chapter 8).

It is easy to set up different addresses for different purposes. Many ISPs give you more than one address and there is no limit to the number of free ones you can use.

MAKING USE OF MAILING LISTS, E-ZINES AND NEWSLETTERS

Mailing lists provide a forum for discussion on a huge range of topics. If you join a mailing list you will have the discussion posted to you as e-mail. This can mean hundreds of items a day!

Joining a mailing list

You have to ask to join a mailing list by 'subscribing' to it, but subscription is free. You will either fill in a form on a web site (this often asks for no more than your e-mail address) or send an e-mail to the relevant address with a message such as 'subscribe' followed by the name of the list you wish to receive.

The first thing you receive is a confirmation of your subscription and details of how to cancel your subsription or 'unsubscribe'. It's important to keep these details so that if you no longer want that information, you can stop it arriving. It's also a good idea to 'unsubscribe' to mailing lists if you're going to be away for some time, otherwise you'll come back to thousands of messages clogging up your post box. It's a bit like remembering to cancel the milk!

Subj: Welcome to green-travel
Date: 15/02/9X 11:43:51
From: Majordom@igc.org
Reply-to: Majordom@igc.org

Welcome to the green-travel mailing list!
Please save this message for future reference. Thank you.

If you ever want to remove yourself from this mailing list, you can send mail to < Majordomo@igc.org > with the following command in the body of your e-mail message:

  unsubscribe green-travel

If you ever need to get in contact with the owner of the list, (if you have trouble unsubscribing, or have questions about the list itself) send e-mail to < owner-green-travel@igc.org >. This is the general rule for most mailing lists when you need to contact a human.

Messages you wish to go to the list should be addressed to:

  green-travel@igc.org

Green-Travel is a moderated internetwork mailing list dedicated to sharing information about environmentally and culturally responsible tourism.

Fig. 46. Green travel's mailing list.

Finding lists

There are directories of mailing lists where you can search for ones related to your interests. Web sites often carry information about related lists, e-zines, newsletters and newsgroups. You can in some

---

I. Your search matched 3 Liszt Select categories:

Business/Travel (1) | Recreation/Travel (9) | Science/Space Travel (2) |

II. Your search matched 6 Liszt Select lists:

INFOTEC-TRAVEL	INFOTEC-TRAVEL - Information Technology in Travel and Tourism Worldwide
kansas	"The on-line home for Kansas fans"
the-rces	List for Discussion of Traveller - The New Era, RCES
TRAVEL-L	Travel-L Discussion of travel experiences
travel	Jewish Travelers Forum
traveller-digest	The Traveller(tm) Mailing List (Digest Version)

III. Your search matched 100 mailing lists:

AAA Travel/Regional Related Web Sites	Travel, adventure travel, regional, holiday, vacation, Europe, USA, Australia

---

Fig. 47. The search result for 'travel' from The Liszt's directory
of 85,714 possibilities.

cases receive a list of lists from automated systems, but it would take forever to read. Searching is much more efficient (see Figure 47).

Different types of lists

Mailing lists are closed or open, moderated or unmoderated:

- closed lists just send information to you

- open mailing lists allow you to contribute to the discussion and can be:

  unmoderated – automatically display all messages posted
  moderated – someone checks the suitability of messages and decides which to include.

Moderation can be useful because it prevents irrelevant, offensive or advertising material creeping in. Most people who act as moderators of lists are unpaid and do it for the love of the subject.

E-zines and newsletters

As well as being available on the web, many e-zines and newsletters can be subscribed to in the same way as mailing lists. Avoid the temptation to subscribe to too many lists and newsletters at once or you'll spend all your time looking at your post and never get away to see the real world.

GETTING THE BEST FROM NEWSGROUPS

Newsgroups are 'places' where people with similar interests exchange views, ask questions, offer help and occasionally bicker and insult each other. There are in excess of 26,000 newsgroups which can be accessed and contributed to by over 40 million people. Hundreds relate to travel and they are a wonderful source of information, amusement and occasionally frustration. Contributors can be experts in their field or weird eccentrics, you should take the same precautions in relation to what you see here as you would with all other parts of the Internet.

Understanding newsgroup names

With such an overwhelming choice you need to know how to select the right newsgroup. Each newsgroup has a unique name made up of several parts. These give you an indication of the subjects they are dealing with and so help you choose appropriate ones.

The first part of the name tells you which category it comes into. Some of the common ones are:

- alt.   Alternative newsgroups. Very much informal and unofficial sources of information. Many travel related newsgroups are in this category.
- biz.   Cover commercial and business matters.
- comp.   Computer related discussion. A good place for tips from experts.
- misc.   A catch-all for subjects that don't fit anywhere else.
- rec.   Most travel-related groups can be found here alongside more sports and hobbies than you ever imagine existed.

The second part of the name gives you an indication of the specific subject they're dealing with. For example:

- alt.travel.uk.air
- rec.travel.misc
- rec. travel. marketplace
- rec.travel.europe
- rec.skiing.resorts.europe

Selecting and subscribing to newsgroups

Newsgroups can be accessed through newsreading software which normally forms part of your Internet connection package. Initially you need to be online to receive the full list of newsgroups kept by your ISP. Receiving this list takes a few minutes, but then you can look at and search it offline. There is usually a facility to search for keywords so you don't have to go through the full 26,000. The number you get access to depends on your ISP.

Subscribing and unsubscribing are simple point and click operations that will be fully explained in the help section of the software you are using. Once you have subscribed new articles will be posted and you collect them each time you go online in the same way that you collect mail. You can, of course, read them offline. There may be hundreds of new articles each day for any one newsgroup, so avoid the temptation to subscribe to lots. Use the help sections of your newsreading software to find out how you can just download message titles to save time and then get the full text of messages that interest you later. If you target the right newsgroup you're more likely to get the right information back.

> We will be in Geneva last week in Jan and first week in Feb. We would like to go to a nearby (2 or 3 hours) resort and ski for the weekend. Can anyone tell us where to go, how to travel, where to stay, so on and so forth. Thanks in advance. <

Not sure about Swiss things but you're only an hours drive from the Mt Blanc area, Chamonix, Megeve, Flaine, Portes du Soleil, La Clusaz etc. It's not much further to the Aosta valley of Italy, Courmayeur, Gressoney etc. In 3 hours you'd be well on the way to the Tarentaise, Val D'Isere, 3 Valleys, Les Arcs etc.

Where to stay? In the past on weekends in between business trips etc I've stayed in Ibis or Mecure hotels in the valleys and just skied wherever looked good in the morning :-)

How to travel? There's a bus from Geneva airport to Chamonix, the web page http://www.chamonix.com/ has some details I think.

Fig. 48. An example from the newsgroup rec.skiing.resorts.europe.

Netiquette

This refers to a loose set of 'rules' on how to behave on the Internet and applies particularly to participation in newsgroups and mailing lists. It basically encourages people to behave in a considerate and intelligent manner. You'll find detailed descriptions of what should and shouldn't be done in the information that comes from your ISP. Take time to acquaint yourself with what is regarded as acceptable behaviour and what is not. The Internet gives you the potential to offend or impress millions!

Frequently asked questions (FAQs)

It's always a good idea to look at the FAQ list before you ask a question because what you need to know may have already been covered. Most newsgroups, mailing lists and even web sites have them.

INTERNET RELAY CHAT

IRC is like a live newsgroup discussion that you can participate in. There are 'channels' where you can 'talk' to other people via your keyboard about a range of subjects including travel. Software which enables you to chat can be obtained from your ISP. Search tools like Yahoo can be used to find organised chat events. Details also appear in TV listings such as *The Guide* in Saturday's *Guardian*.

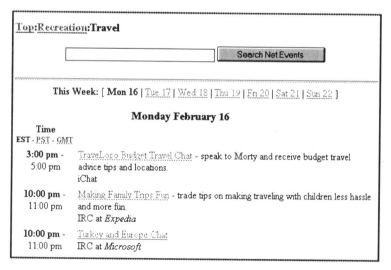

Fig. 49. Yahoo's travel chat events.

WORKING OFFLINE

The time you spend online always has a cost attached to it. This could be the cost of phone calls, provider charges, or the value of your own time. Time somehow changes its shape once you become absorbed in what you are doing. You follow links and get interested in what's there, and the ten minutes you'd intended to spend looking something up has transformed itself into three hours.

You can significantly reduce the time you spend online by always reading and printing documents whilst offline. Any document you view is stored in the computer's memory cache for a time. The help section of your web browser software will tell you how to regulate the size and content of it and what its limitations are. You can open these files without being connected to the phone. They have unappealing names such as m0q3812.htm, but you can save them as something more meaningful using the File Save As... command. This will save a document but not any links you follow unless you save them separately.

Offline reading software

The newest (version 4) browsers incorporate offline reading facilities, but you may need to use extra software to view offline if you are using an older browser, or if you want to save more files than your cache has space for. Offline browsers are widely available, and make the process of looking at sites visited previously a lot easier. They process the cache into an index which retains the original file names and URLs, and allows you to follow any links that you made whilst online.

This software can easily be obtained as freeware or shareware downloaded from the Web. You can find details of what's available using a search engine or one of the shareware sites.

HINTS AND TIPS FOR COST-EFFECTIVE INTERNET USE

Use the free trials that Internet Service Providers offer before you decide who to sign up with.
There can be a significant difference in the time information transfers take with different ISPs. A range of different subscription packages is available. Restricted time is always cheaper than unlimited access and worth considering if you know you are likely to just use it for a few hours a month. If, however, you go over the agreed number of hours, the charges per extra hour can be high.

Call discount schemes
If you pay for local calls, check whether your phone company has a scheme for offering discounts on frequently called numbers and add the ISP's internet access number to it. Cable companies may provide telephone services that offer some free local calls.

Use the Internet when it's cheap and fast
Only access the web during cheap rate for phone calls, and try to do most of your searching at times that are not busy. This varies depending where you live, but it's basically governed by whether the largest user, the USA, is asleep or awake. At busy times you may fail to make connections and data transfer will be slower.

Access sites through bookmarks
Create bookmarks offline so that time online is not spent typing in long URLs. Bookmarks (also known as Hot Lists and Favorites) can be arranged in folders and moved around. Have the ones you next want to visit at the top of your bookmark file. Explore the facilities available for managing bookmark files offline using the appropriate browser help section.

Avoid slow-loading home pages
A site's home page is not always the best one to bookmark as your future starting point for revisits. Many take a long time to load, subsequent pages are usually plainer and give access to the rest of the site. Where access is via a password it is often possible to bookmark later pages in the site and go straight to them.

Stop images, sound and video clips being loaded automatically
Instruct your browser not to load these. All browsers have an option to turn automatic loading on and off, details will be in their help sections. Pages without images take less time to load. The picture is replaced by the ⬛ icon. Clicking on this will load the picture.

On well designed sites you are told what the picture is and in some cases how big the file is. You can load images for the whole page using the image icon in the toolbar. Figure 50 shows a mixture of text and images, making the page usable without images. Other less thoughtfully constructed sites present a full screen of image icons and no text, in which case you need to load images before you can make use of it. Some sites allow you to load text only versions from their home page. They're not as pretty, but they have all the same information.

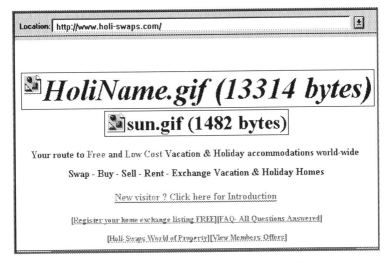

Fig. 50. A web page with images turned off.

Don't try to read information whilst online
Go quickly to any links that interest you, your eye will be drawn to them because they are coloured and underlined text or pictures. Watch the status bar which tells you what's happening with your connections and data transfer. Once it says Document Done, or words to that effect, it has cached the link you requested and you can go back to where you started using the Back button. Do the same with all the other useful links. (If you hit the Back button before it's all loaded you get a message telling you the transfer has been interrupted. You end up with an incomplete document and will need to reload.) Use offline browser software to read pages and evaluate their usefulness.

Print out information whilst offline
Read it at your leisure with a highlighter pen to hand. Mark any links you want to visit and add them to the top of your bookmark file offline, ready for when you next connect.

Compose all your e-mail messages offline
You can store messages in an out tray with most mail software. No matter how many messages you have and how diverse their destinations they will all be sent as part of the same phone call.

Use the address book facility to store frequently used addresses. Amend this offline.

Copy and paste e-mail for web-based accounts
If you are using a free e-mail account and cannot compose offline, write your message using a word processing package, copy it to the clipboard. Then go online, access your e-mail host and paste the message in.

Plan ahead
Have a clear idea of what you hope to get from a session on the Internet before you connect. Have e-mails ready to send and sites you want to visit at the top of your bookmark list. If you know that you're likely to get carried away, set a timer to jolt you out of your absorption.

Keep an eye on downloads
When downloading software check the size of the files and estimate the time the transfer is likely to take. This will depend on your hardware, the various linking connections and the time of day. Once a program is downloading it usually runs a clock to show you how long it will take; if that's too long, cancel it. If you decide to do a long download, don't go away and leave it. Keep checking that data is still coming through and that the clock is counting down. If something goes wrong, the data transfer can stop, but you are still paying for the telephone connection.

Only use the Internet when it's appropriate
Don't assume that the Internet is the best way to research everything. Some pages are only a reproduction of what is available, sometimes for free, in printed form or as a computer program. Some travel company sites, for example, may just be showing their brochure that is available for no cost in your local travel agents.

Give up when you're losing
Both telephones and computers are a wonderful tools when they work properly, and sources of immense frustration when they don't. Their complexity means that there will inevitably be times when things go wrong. If things aren't working properly, it's a good idea to take a break. It may be fixed by the time you come back.

SITESEEING TIPS

Free and cheap software

http://www.shareware.com
http://www.download.com
Both are sites where you can search for and download software. Make sure you have an up-to-date virus checker or download one from here.

Unmozify
http://www.evolve.co.uk
Read about and download this useful offline browsing software.

Free e-mail providers
Many of the search engines and directories listed in Chapter 2 offer free e-mail. Other providers include:

http://www.hotmail.com
http://www.rocketmail.com

Mail forwarders

http://www.iname.com
http://www.netforward.com
http://www.myownemail.com

All have a large selection of interesting aliases that are yours to keep forever. You can have lots of fun creating a new identity!

Searchable directories of mailing lists

http://www.liszt.com
http://www.neosoft.com/internet/paml

Both the above will find, categorise, describe and give details of how to subscribe to lists.

Searchable directories of newsgroups

http://www.dejanews.com
A searchable archive of postings to newsgroups. Good for reading old articles and getting a feel for what different groups are about.

Newsgroup postings can be also searched for on Alta Vista, HotBot, Excite and Yahoo (listed in Chapter 8).

Finding e-mail addresses

http://www.whowhere.com

Has an e-mail finding facility as do most search engines. You can submit your address to any of these if you want it made public.

Glossary

Bit. Short for 'binary digit', it is the smallest unit of information stored on a computer. The speed at which a modem transfers data is measured in bit per second (bps).

Bookmark. A stored URL that gives you subsequent access to that site with a single click of the mouse. Other names for this include **hotlist** and **favourite place**.

Browser. Software that enables you to view documents on the web.

Cache. Stores the information downloaded from the Internet on your computer. This enables you to reload quickly on subsequent visits and to look at pages offline.

Cybercafé. A café with computers where you can eat, drink and access the Internet. A growing phenomenon.

Download. Transfer of information from a computer on the Internet to your own computer.

E-mail. Short for electronic mail. A system for sending messages and files from one Internet linked computer to another.

Encryption. Writing messages in coded form to ensure they can be read only by recipients who have the key to that code.

FAQ. Frequently Asked Question. Web sites and newsgroups have lists of these to help you make good use of what they offer (and to prevent you being a nuisance by asking something that's already been asked thousands of times).

Freeware. Software that is completely free.

FTP. File Transfer Protocol. A method of transferring files from one computer to another.

Fuzzy logic. Used by some search engines to look for words that are misspelled.

Gateway sites. Contain links to large numbers of other sites on a particular topic.

Hard disc. The disc inside your computer where most of the information is stored. Floppy discs are a smaller version of this and can be used to copy and move files between computers.

Hits. The total number of visits to a web site.

HTML. Hyper Text Markup Language. The computer language in which web pages are written. You don't need to understand it unless you want to write web pages of your own. To see what it looks like go to View Document Source for any web page.

Hypertext link. An image or piece of text on a web page that provides a link to another site or document.

Internet. A worldwide network of linked computers.

Internet relay chat (IRC). A 'live' discussion on the Internet where users talk by typing messages to each other.

Internet service provider (ISP). The organisation that provides you with Internet access.

Lurker. A person who reads news or chat group material without joining in.

Metacrawler. A program that allows a search to be sent to several search engines and directories.

Modem. The device that connects your computer to the phone network.

Netiquette. Internet etiquette. A loose set of 'rules' about how to behave when using the Internet which particularly applies to newsgroups.

Newsgroup. An Internet discussion group. There are groups for every topic imaginable.

Offline browser. Software which allows you to view previously accessed web pages and links without connecting to the Internet.

Online. Connected to the Internet via the phone network.

Point of presence (POP). The phone number that connects you to your ISP.

Search engine/directory. A facility that acts as an index to the Internet and allows you to search for relevant documents. Engines are compiled by robots, directories by humans.

Secure sockets layer (SSL). Internet security system which encodes the data you send so no one can read or change it during transmission. Financial transactions and transfer of other sensitive data should be done only through secure sites.

Shareware. Software that can be tried out for free for a limited period. Continued use requires a fee to be paid to the author.

Uniform resource locator (URL). The address of a web site. Every web page has a unique URL.

Virus. A virus is designed to disrupt the working of a computer. It can be transferred from one computer to another. It is essential to install software that checks for viruses before you download anything from the web. If you have a virus it may also be 'cleaned up' by this software.

Web page. A document viewed on the web. It can be several paper pages long.

Web site. A collection of web pages.

World wide web. The most widely used part of the Internet. It allows publication of and access to documents. Also referred to as WWW, W3 and the web.

Further Reading

Most of the reading you need to do on travel and Internet use can be done via the Internet, but sometimes it's nicer to read a real book. Details of travel books are contained in Chapter 2. The following are useful resources for learning more about Internet use and its applications.

BOOKS

ABC's of Microsoft Internet Explorer 3, John Ross (Sybex 1996).
ABC's of Microsoft Internet Explorer 4, John Ross (Sybex 1997).
Netscape and WWW for Dummies, P Hoffman (IDG Books World).
Net That Job, Irene Krechowiecka (Kogan Page 1998).
Rough Guide to The Internet & World Wide Web, Angus Kennedy (Rough Guides 1997).

MAGAZINES

Internet Magazine.
PC World.

Index of Sites Listed

Main Index

MANAGING YOUR FIRST COMPUTER
How to perform core tasks and go on to achieve proficiency

Carol Dolman and Marcus Saunders

Anyone new to the world of computers can expect to be baffled by the huge array of equipment, programs, books, and above all, the mind-boggling jargon that goes with the territory. How much do you need to know to use a computer effectively? This book will guide the first-time or inexperienced user simply and painlessly towards making use of all major applications in the shortest possible time. With clear illustrations and practical exercises, the reader will be using their computer effectively right from the start. Carol Dolman and Marcus Saunders are both qualified computer technicians who have worked with computers since 1979. They run their own computer business, servicing and installing computer systems, and specialise in instructing those new to computing.

144pp. illus. 1 85703 293 4.

CREATING A WEB SITE
How to build a web site in a weekend and keep it in good shape

Bruce Durie

Anyone can have a Web site and anyone can design one – you don't have to be a computer wizard. All you need is a standard multimedia PC, a modem, some basic software, a few good ideas, a design and some free time. Whether you want your own home page, a site for your school, club, church or group, small business or major company, this book will provide you with the know-how to create your own Web site quickly, using step-by-step instructions. Bruce Durie works in education and has written hundreds of articles for a variety of publications including *New Scientist*, plus books and plays. He has constructed a number of Web sites both for clients and for his own amusement.

144pp. illus. 1 85703 356 6.